King
Persp
SER

Territory
OF THE
Kingdom

REVEALING THE FRAMEWORK
OF OUR INHERITANCE

Alan J. Osborn

Book Series website is www.kingdomperspective.net
Published by Osborn Publishing, Ramsgate, England
Cover Design by Annika Mai Kreitsman

ISBN 978-1-913858-00-1

First Edition, Revision C. First Printed in England Dec., 2020.

Dedication

This, my first book, is dedicated to

my spiritual parents:

John and Trish Waller

Acknowledgements

Much of the resource used in part one of this series has of course been the guiding and inspiration of the Holy Spirit, but there are some particular people to highlight and honour…

Kevin J. McManus. You and your family left home in Texas to come and serve and support me in extending the Kingdom, as part of Elim Oasis Church in Broadstairs, England. You served Jesus with all you had and were pivotal in helping our local mission, Impact England, to become a reality. You were a good and faithful 'all in' servant. I miss you my friend and brother in Christ. As you live eternally now with Jesus, I hope you have that basketball court ready for the game we never got to play. In our last conversation, you offered to help me in any way you could, to put this Kingdom series together. Boy, I wish you were here to do so! I guess God wanted me to do it. I hope that you are pleased with this first result.

Dan Allen, Pastor of Leon Springs Baptist Church in San Antonio, Texas. You opened up your home, allowing me time and space to focus on my church vision, and you also sent the first Impact England mission team to us in Broadstairs.

Alan Poole. For your friendship, reviews and feedback, and your prayer support.

Roy and Lainey Hitchman. I could not have got as far as this publication, if it had not been for your love and support, as well as your knowledge and experience of the self-publishing world.

Geoff Richardson. For both reviewing my manuscripts and challenging my thinking about the Church and the Kingdom.

My close friends and family. You have read and reviewed the draft versions of this book and have provided much-needed encouragement and extremely helpful feedback. Thank you.

Preface

At the outset of this first book, my overall goal is to produce a four-part series covering the four component parts of the Kingdom. It is my hope and prayer that each book will be a helpful stand-alone resource to the Body of Christ, whilst retaining its vital part in the broader understanding of living from a 'Kingdom Perspective'. In other words, each book will be an important, individual piece in a four-piece jigsaw.

Later will come books on the '*Citizens of the Kingdom*', the '*Laws of the Kingdom*' and finally, the '*King of the Kingdom*'; but I'm starting with the '*Territory of the Kingdom*'. This is because I believe it will be helpful first to put up a framework of understanding that gives us the broader concepts, before delving into the other three components. **It is essential that the Kingdom is formed within us as disciples of Jesus, so that it can be extended through us.** Getting a handle on its territory helps us to begin to grasp, describe and live in this 'hard to see' Kingdom. I will build the series through the citizens and laws, that we do perhaps need greater clarity of, before ultimately reaching its pinnacle: Jesus the King!

This first book will cover the territory of the Kingdom and aims to answer a variety of common questions like: How do I enter the Kingdom? Where and when is this Kingdom? How will people respond to the message of the Kingdom? What is the Kingdom like? How is the Kingdom unlocked and made accessible? Is hell a real place? What is heaven going to be like?

I am not aiming to become a deep theologian or an academic writer, but rather to take something that is either complex, misunderstood or somehow hidden from our understanding, and bring it with a new level of clarity, to the forefront of our thinking, so that **the main thing Jesus spoke about, becomes the main thing that we speak about**. When I learnt about these four aforementioned components of any and every Kingdom, they suddenly allowed me to see a way of framing things for a clearer understanding. This also enabled me to begin my own journey of discovery into each one. I had no idea where this would take me or what the results would be, either for me personally or for the church I lead. Yet, it seemed to be the right direction in which to head.

I am still journeying and still learning! I may never be able to fully grasp all that the Kingdom is and means, but I am enjoying the adventure and felt that it could be helpful for you to be able to see with a 'Kingdom Perspective' too.

I have at least now discovered one important thing: that I must preach the Kingdom... *"Jesus said, I must preach the good news of the Kingdom of God to the other towns also, **because that is why I was sent**"* (Luke 4:43).

Welcome to the Kingdom of Heaven!

Foreword

Alan and I have been friends for the past 20 years, having first met him when worshiping at the Elim Pentecostal Church in Windsor, England, on my return visits from the USA. Just prior to that, after being prompted by the Holy Spirit, I suggested that we become prayer partners. Until both he and I later moved away, we met up regularly every fortnight for prayer, and still today, via the wonders of technology, we pray over the Internet from time to time. With a bond of friendship I can only describe as incredible, Alan has been faithful and dependable and over the years. We have both individually been through a lot, and without the prayer partnership I do not think either of us would have been on the faith journeys we have travelled. It has been a real privilege to share and due to the common denominator being our faith and committed prayer lives, we have seen each other develop in ministry. We tackled many subjects from mundane and personal matters to serious topics and difficult theological issues.

In particular, I have seen Alan grow from a reserved worship leader to an extremely accomplished one; as we met over the years and prayed, Alan's journey into God grew enormously and it was soon evident that he was destined for full-time ministry, which I fully endorsed and encouraged. As Alan has developed from lay ministry into the ordained minister he is today, and from leading his church, taking missions teams abroad and hosting them locally. It is clear he has always had a passion for the Kingdom, making disciples and bringing the Gospel to people. That has transformed his thinking as well as impacting his own journey into God. Knowing the only possible way forward was through the power of prayer (something dear to my own heart), this has become a priority of his own life and the church's ministry. Prayer has allowed the Holy Spirit to empower and guide Alan in all he does.

I know every book has its unique features, but tackling the 'Territory of the Kingdom' is probably in a category by itself. In reading the 'Territory of the Kingdom', I found it is a subject not widely addressed generally. I believe it has been written with a real passion and with words fueled by the Holy Spirit to demonstrate how we need to live with a Kingdom perspective. He challenges the reader to make the necessary changes in their daily walk with Jesus. Alan has used vocabulary that is easily understood, communicates transformational truth, and also highlights Kingdom perspectives more clearly and directly than perhaps by other authors. It is one thing to write on a subject, it is another to be a living demonstration of what you share. It is evident in his words and in his life, that Alan reveals the powerful effect that the relentless pursuit of God's purpose produces.

As it is noted in the Epilogue, now that the framework of the 'Territory of the Kingdom' has been established, it is time to ponder, what does it mean for each reader personally? Without the power of God that is so obviously present in Alan's life and ministry, we might not only be reading extended transcripts from his sermons, but also, because of the revelation received through the Holy Spirit, true gems of spiritual insight shine through the pages that are penned in this book. This book certainly questions traditional thinking, confronts our casual complacency, challenges our pre-conceptions or lack of understanding about the Territory of the Kingdom. It is a fresh resource for individuals or groups who may wish to study Jesus' parables in Matthew.

As you read through this book and hopefully the further books in the series to follow, I pray that your territory will also be enlarged... *"Oh, that you would bless me and enlarge my territory! Let your hand be with me"* (1 Chron. 4:10), that your response to the call will be positive and your discipleship to Jesus will be turned upside down, in order to become an active participant in the Kingdom, moving out of your comfort zone and grasping this Kingdom perspective.

Alan Poole MDiv: MBA: ACIS: FIAC: BCom (Hon)

Contents

SECTION ONE – Introducing the Kingdom

SECTION TWO – The Kingdom of Heaven is Like…

SECTION THREE – Additional Kingdom Concepts

Introducing the Kingdom

CHAPTER ONE

How my Kingdom Journey Began

I first met Steve Sameniego back in 2006, when he visited the church I was then part of, The Ark Community Church[1] in Watford, England. We 'clicked' straight away, and as brothers in Christ, we found we had some things in common. He lived in Texas, and I had spent a year of my schooling in Houston, completing Junior High. I had retained a soft spot for Texas, and after returning to England, I finished school at sixteen, leaving to become an aircraft engineering apprentice. I learnt to manufacture ejector seats for military aircraft. Steve had been a US fighter pilot and could well have sat in one of the seats I had in some small way helped to produce. We both, at that point, also worked full time in the IT industry.

We had children of similar ages, and so Steve invited us to holiday and stay with them in San Antonio. If I could make a much-longed-for walk down memory lane, to revisit Cairns west of Houston, to show my children where I had lived and spent a year of my childhood, then I could incorporate a stay with Steve and his family. That simple chat over a cuppa (you know how Brits love a cup of tea!) and an invite to visit, helped lead me to what I believe was a new God-given path for my life, not to mention that of our children's lives. In 2013, my son Carl married Steve's daughter Carly and they both now live in San

---

[1] See thearkcc.org.

Antonio. Steve and I now share two beautiful granddaughters, Lucy and Eleanor, at this time of writing. It is as I am sat on the very back row, flying over to Texas with my wife Alice, to meet Eleanor for the very first time, that these first words are being penned – or should I say typed.

In January of 2015, I went to Costa Rica on a mission trip called Impacto Costa Rica. By this time, Steve had pioneered an organisation called Vital Seed Ministries[2] to help believers run and grow businesses according to biblical and Kingdom principles. Vital Seed had also broadened to help expand the Kingdom through overseas missions. Impact Missions had been born. As for me, I had gone down the route of Pastoral Ministry. I had been ordained as a minister in the Elim Pentecostal Movement[3] in the UK. Having served as a bi-vocational Assistant Pastor, Associate Pastor and then Acting Pastor in my first church[4], in a place called Lane End, I was waiting to transfer into my second church, when I was fortunate enough to join with this particular mission.

Steve's mantra was to "seek first the Kingdom" based on Matthew 6:33, and had been since I had known him. This talk of the Kingdom had caught my attention because, I had to admit, even though I had been a Christian for over twenty-five years and was now a Pastor, I really did not understand nor was able to grasp what the Kingdom really meant. What does heaven on earth actually mean?

---

[2] See vitalseed.org.

[3] See elim.org.

[4] See elimhopechurch.net.

Back to Impacto Costa Rica. During the mission I spoke briefly, along with some others, at a pastors' and leaders' conference for those living and ministering in the town of Liberia. It was there that I heard for the first time, through the ministry of Pastor Randy Boyd of Prepare International Ministries[5], that every Kingdom has four key components: **territory, citizens, laws** and a **King.** It was a concept that I could not shake off, and something I knew that was going to be key for both my future, and also for that of the next church I would end up leading. Take the United Kingdom for example: its territory is made up of England, Wales, Scotland and Northern Ireland; its citizens are around sixty-three million people of which I am one; its laws exist and are made and passed in Parliament, being upheld by the justice systems law courts; and its King, well, that's currently a Queen: Elizabeth II is our longest ever serving monarch. In the same way, the Kingdom of God has a territory which is this world that Jesus stepped into. It also has citizens who are the disciples of Jesus, laws which are based on Jesus' Sermon on the Mount, and a King who is also Jesus!

This four-component concept seemed so basic and obvious; how could it have been missed? Yet I, then close to completing my Master of Arts degree in Theology, did not have any real grasp of this Kingdom stuff. Was that the fault of my church's programmes during the time spent within them, or was it the fault of my Bible College? Now, first let me say, that I have loved every church I have been part of, and that I also count it a real privilege to have been educated at the excellent Regents

---

[5] See prepareinternational.org.

Theological College[6] in Malvern, England. Without abdicating any of my own responsibility, I do wonder if it is perhaps both! Please let me explain. The Church generally is not teaching about the Kingdom in a focused way, and so, to some extent, assumes there is an understanding of, and a full allegiance to, the King and his Kingdom. We need to improve our focus to help us make disciples. At Bible College, there was never a module to take, assignment to complete, or exam to sit, about this topic. I do wonder why? Perhaps it is too large a subject or field of study? Of course, in both of these environments the Kingdom was mentioned, but never was it at the forefront of teaching; so to me personally, it all remained a bit of a mystery.

It is because I soon realised that my lack of understanding was not unique to me, that I felt compelled to write this series: to provide some clarity for believers in Jesus everywhere, helping others to also be able to piece together the jigsaw that Jesus left us. Our churches and theological institutions may never provide us with a clear picture of the very thing that Jesus our King spoke about and demonstrated most, when he was physically here on earth.

It was at this same conference that I met and became good friends with Pastor Rafael Gutiérrez, who leads Iglesia Puerta de Restauracion[7] or Door of Restoration Church. Rafael has more than just a wonderfully infectious influence in making disciples, through teaching them to know and practice the laws

---

[6] See regents-tc.ac.uk.
[7] See puertaderestauracion.com.

of the Kingdom, he is anointed to do so. His friendship and insights have been invaluable.

During a time of praying alone on that mission trip, God spoke to me about the 'mission' for the church that I would go on to lead. "*Discipleship for Mission*" is what he said. Later in 2015, I went on to pastor Elim Oasis Church[8] in Broadstairs, and this immediately became our church tagline. It is the **'why'**, or the reason that our local expression of church exists, to make disciples that also see themselves as missionaries! As I said, it was a pivotal mission trip for me.

These events led me to begin a strategy for learning and teaching about the Kingdom. I spent a lot of time in 2016, thinking and praying about the vision and direction that I believed God had for us as a church. When this was released to the church at the beginning of 2017, we had an initial four-year vision through to 2020. It seemed a sensible approach to use each year to bring a main preaching series, focusing on one of the Kingdom components, to underpin our "why?"

This book series is the result of those preaching efforts and the understanding God has given me on this journey. I am still learning and simply desire to help paint a clearer picture, to help bring revelation of what it actually means to live from a Kingdom Perspective, but to do so on a very practical level, exploring **'how'** we can live out our faith in Jesus, with a heavenly perspective rather than purely an earthly one.

---

[8] See elimoasischurch.com.

CHAPTER TWO

Discovering the Kingdom

I thought it would be helpful to start with a very quick biblical discovery of the Kingdom. There are many scripture references in brackets to show you where you can find them. Please do feel free to read on and simply skip over them as you go, but for some, they will be more helpful being included; and they can also be used for a deeper discussion with others in small groups, for example. But I will highlight the key points for you.

In the Old Testament (OT) we see that God the Father, who is the 'Ancient of Days', hands his Kingdom over to the 'Son of Man' who is his Son Jesus, **making Jesus its King** (Dan. 7:13-14). We also see in Daniel, as well as in the Psalms, that this Kingdom is an **everlasting** Kingdom, that **displays his mighty acts and his glorious splendour** (Dan. 7:14, 27; Psalm 145:9-13). It is also referred to as an **eternal** Kingdom (Dan. 4:3, 34b [also in 2 Peter 1:11]).

In the New Testament (NT) there are different terms used for the Kingdom, for example: the Kingdom of God, the Kingdom of Heaven, the Kingdom of his Son or the Son he loves (Col. 1:13), my Father's Kingdom (Matt. 26:29), the Kingdom of Christ and of God (Eph. 5:5), the Kingdom of light (Col. 1:12), his Kingdom (1 Thes. 2:12; 2 Tim. 4:1), his heavenly Kingdom (2 Tim. 4:18), etc. These terms are synonymous and so are used to describe the same thing. They all refer to the same single Kingdom which is God's Kingdom and his rule on earth.

The reason why the original authors used different terms, was to assist the various cultures that they were writing into, to help them better understand and grasp the meaning.

We find that the Kingdom of Heaven was **the first thing that Jesus preached**... *"Repent, for the kingdom of heaven is at hand"* (Matt. 4:17) or *"the Kingdom of God is near"* (Mark 1:15). This same message is also what John the Baptist **his forerunner preached** (Matt. 3:2); and what Jesus later sent out the **disciples to preach** (Matt. 10:7); and to **display** his mighty acts by healing the sick, raising the dead, cleansing those who have leprosy and by driving out demons (Matt. 10:8). This Kingdom is good news, that can and must be proclaimed and displayed today! It is not passive but an active Kingdom, that we are **authorised to demonstrate** and that Jesus expects us to **freely give away!** On this point of us demonstrating the power of the Kingdom, we also see this affirmed by the Apostle Paul: the Kingdom is not just... *"a matter of talk but of **power**"* (1 Cor. 4:20). The Apostle John concurs writing... *"now have come the salvation and the **power** and the kingdom of our God"* (Rev. 12:10).

We know that we have been rescued from the dominion of darkness and **brought into the Kingdom** of the Son he loves (Col. 1:12-13). The Kingdom is **the first thing that we must seek** (Matt. 6:33), and we are to **pray for this Kingdom to come on the earth**, just like it is in heaven (Matt. 6:10). But did you know, that we can all become **great in the Kingdom by practising and teaching its laws** (Matt. 5:19), and that by doing this, our righteousness will surpass that of the Pharisees and the teachers of the law, which is a pre-requisite of entry (Matt. 5:20)?

The Kingdom is a place where **faith and love increase** and **we are indeed worthy of it** – particularly if we persevere in faith even when we go through life's trials, persecution and suffering (2 Thes. 1:3-5). We are not simply invited to be part of the Kingdom and 'that's all folks!' Being part of this incredible Kingdom should transform every part of us. It is a place of **pure living, of peace and joy**, and it **cannot exclude the Holy Spirit** (Rom. 14:17). We have been **given the keys** to the Kingdom, to unlock and to use our spiritual authority (Matt. 16:19); and when we have entered it, we can receive the **knowledge of its secrets** (Matt. 13:11; Mark 4:11).

The Kingdom **requires unity** (Matt. 12:25-26), and we are to **extend it** by **making disciples** (Matt. 28:18-20) of those who can then **make further disciples** (2 Tim. 2:2). We keep on doing this until the day that **Jesus hands the Kingdom back to the Father** (1 Cor. 15:24).

The Kingdom was the first thing Jesus preached, **the number one thing that he taught about**; he even spoke about it after his resurrection (Acts 1:3). I have to wonder though – what is the one thing that followers of Jesus talk most about today? What is your most frequent social media post typically about? The Kingdom was the central theme of Jesus, and so surely, it should also be our central theme too.

Let's begin to think more about and ponder the Kingdom, so that we can describe it and demonstrate it to others. It is comprised of: 1) the **territory** of this world, 2) **citizens** who are disciples of Jesus, 3) **laws** found in the Sermon on the Mount, and 4) **King** Jesus.

CHAPTER THREE

Entry into the Kingdom

I hope that the short introduction to the Kingdom has stirred something within you. So, are you in, or are you not? Does everyone who attends church on Sunday automatically enter or can anyone join?

I would say that scripture does leave entry to the Kingdom open to all of humanity, even though God knows all things and therefore who will choose to enter... *"I say to you that many will come from the east and the west, and will take their places at the feast with Abraham, Isaac and Jacob in the kingdom of heaven"* (Matt. 8:11). Luke also adds from the *"North and South"* (Luke 13:29).

Entry into the Kingdom is not like joining a club. There is no official membership even if our churches or denominations choose to have one. Rather, **entry is for great purpose**, and for living the most fulfilling and noble life one can on this earth. To live under the blessings (Matt. 5:3-12) and covering of the King of kings (1 Tim. 6:15; Rev. 17:14; 19:16), and to be part of extending the wonders of heaven on this earth. It is not meant to be a ticket to heaven that we put in our pocket until we depart this world. It should bring total transformation to us in everything, and therefore into each of our spheres of influence, as well as our relationships and our friendships. Scripture does appear to give us some further guidance on: 1) how to enter, 2) some expected ongoing requirements, and 3) who it is for.

How does One Enter?

Firstly, to become a follower of Jesus a person needs to truly believe within them that he is actually who he claimed to be, i.e. God, and to **confess** this (Rom. 10:9-10). In this, both **repentance** (turning from living our way to living God's way) and **faith** in Jesus, are required for entrance to the Kingdom. Another word for this is, of course, **salvation**.

Secondly, a person must be **born again** or born of the Holy Spirit to be able to see the Kingdom (John 3:3, 5). If we have become alive in Christ (Rom. 6:1-14) we can interact directly from within our spirit, with the Holy Spirit. We talk to and hear from God! It is, therefore, a spiritual Kingdom that is governed in the spiritual realm, so that we know what God wants us to do for him, in this earthly realm. Paul confirms this... *"I declare to you, brothers and sisters, that flesh and blood cannot inherit the kingdom of God, nor does the perishable inherit the imperishable"* (1 Cor. 15:50).

As a Pentecostal Pastor, I would suggest that all followers of Jesus explore, accept and run towards, what is known as the Baptism in the Holy Spirit. Simply put, accepting Jesus brings the Holy Spirit to reside within us as a small flame. The word baptism means to be fully immersed into something; and so, one way to look at this is to turn up the small flame into a roaring fire. This is what brings us such great intimacy with God from within our spirit, and a much greater desire to know and to worship him, as well as a heightened or an increased ability to hear from him. This is a significant factor in being able to both **obey** and **display** the majestic and powerful nature of his Kingdom to others.

Therefore, to be truly effective in this spiritual Kingdom, we need the fullness of the Holy Spirit within us, **just as Jesus had** at his water baptism (Matt. 3:16).

The Four-Square Gospel sees Jesus at the Saviour, Healer, Coming King and the Baptiser in the Holy Spirit (John 1:33). The latter is where our empowerment comes from, and the strength to serve God. How else could we attempt to fulfil our mandate to make disciples of all nations? It is 'as we go' that Jesus promises to be with us (Matt. 28:20) and he achieves this through the Holy Spirit living inside of us (Rom. 8:11). Jesus worked in perfect harmony with the Father and the Holy Spirit (being 'full of' and 'led by'), throughout his earthly life and ministry. The same Holy Spirit is the means by which we too, as disciples today, can both witness and demonstrate the power of the Kingdom (Acts 1:8).

Any Christian, or church gathering, can become full of the Holy Spirit if they simply are willing. All that is required is the desire, and to ask. Those that do will be able to function in the gifts of the Spirit, and also to grow more ably in the fruit of the Spirit. As the Kingdom was central to Jesus teaching, so the Holy Spirit remains central to advancing the Kingdom today, as we preach the gospel until we reach all nations.

Thirdly, we do know that it is hard for the rich to enter the Kingdom (Matt. 19:16-24; Mark 10:17-25; Luke 18:24-25), because many people do not see the need for it when they have their primary needs of shelter, food and warmth met as well as material luxuries. What they can and often do easily miss, or not understand, is their need for spiritual fulfilment. This is only found through relationship with the living God.

Finally, entry to the Kingdom (Matt. 10:23-24) is synonymous with 'eternal life' (Matt. 10:30). We will look a little deeper at eternal life later in the chapter on heaven.

What does Entry Require of Us?

In essence, it is to practise its laws and teach them to others. Practice is something done so frequently, that we become so familiar with living the laws ourselves, that we can teach them to others. Practicing is not something that we do in order that we might earn or gain reward, but it is something we lovingly and obediently do, because we know that his laws will enable us to love him and to love others as ourselves (Matt. 22:37-40).

It is only when Jesus places his robe of righteousness over us at salvation (known as, justification), that we can then surpass the righteousness of the Pharisees and the teachers of the law, which is a pre-requisite of entry (Matt. 5:20). Entrance requires a level of righteousness that only results from God's reign within us, so we simply cannot achieve this ourselves. The King incredibly provides that which is demanded of us. Once in, we must then begin to be and act like Jesus. Little by little, as we live out his laws, we put this 'right living' into practice and journey through an inward change, for the rest of our time here on this earth (that is, sanctification).

The Kingdom also requires that we do the will of the Father, regardless of the personal cost (Matt. 7:21; 21:28-31). For that we need to read his written word, the Bible, and to be able to hear his spoken voice as well, like a sheep hears its shepherd (John 10:27); and then we must actually obey him!

Those in, are required to become like a child in their purity of heart (Matt. 18:1-5; Mark 10:15; Luke 18:17), and to produce fruit with whatever resources they may have (Matt. 21:33-43). This includes fruit within a person, which is known as the fruit of the Spirit (Gal. 5:22-23). Again, this can only come through an intimate relationship with the Holy Spirit (Gal. 5:25).

We have got some ongoing work to do, to enable this inward change, so that we can be Jesus outwardly to others.

Who is the Kingdom For?

The Beatitudes tell us that the Kingdom is for the poor in spirit (Matt. 5:3) and those persecuted because of righteousness (Matt. 5:10). This relates to those who know that they are poor in spirit without the Holy Spirit, and therefore they rely on him, and to those who suffer persecution because they live as a living example of the Kingdom.

Persecution can take many forms, from the persecuted church around the world that faces death for their faith in Jesus, to being bullied in the factory, or the teenage school girl or boy standing firm in their faith, despite the emotional rejection they might face from their peers.

The Kingdom is for those who are rich in faith (James 2:5). How rich is your faith? We seek riches in many places and many things. Living actively in the Kingdom is for those who are stepping out in faith and trusting God in every way possible.

As we close this chapter, a word of warning for those who are in. Sin does not suddenly cease to exist for us. It can, however, prevent us from enjoying the fullness of this most incredible Kingdom (1 Cor. 6:9-10; Gal. 5:19-21; Eph. 5:5) if we continue to succumb to its desires.

CHAPTER FOUR

Where and When is this Kingdom?

The meta-narrative, or the big picture, of the Bible is for the union of heaven and earth; God and people. The focus of the Bible is for us to live out the Kingdom here on earth, that Jesus ushered in and made a reality. It is not only the place where we will one day end up! There is less detail in the Bible about the future Kingdom (heaven), which is why there are so many ideas about it and the end times. Yes, we are supposed to be intrigued by these things, but keep our main focus on living with and for the King, and being those who touch this earthly realm with the things of heaven. We are on earth, but should be living with a heavenly focus i.e. with a Kingdom Perspective.

We do live in this overlapping age of heaven and earth. Let me explain: we are not in the beginning age of how things were created, nor are we yet in the age when all things will become new. Our assignment, should you choose to accept it, is to extend the influence of the heavenly Kingdom across this earthly realm, in this present age.

Where is this Kingdom?

The message of the Kingdom being 'at hand' is key, and is for us to use as we go and reach out to a lost world. But what does that really mean? Could this mean in our physical hands? If we held up our hands together and your hand is bigger than mine does that mean you have more of the Kingdom? If that was the case, I would be out buying one of those large foam number one hands used to support your favourite team at the game! No, it means the Kingdom is within people's reach, all around and within their grasp if they desire it.

It is within You

The Kingdom is not something you have to hunt or search for according to Luke… *"Once, having been asked by the Pharisees when the kingdom of God would come, Jesus replied, "The kingdom of God does not come with your careful observation nor will people say, 'Here it is,' or 'There it is,' because **the kingdom of God is within you**""* (Luke 17:20-21). Jesus is asked by the religious Pharisees when the Kingdom of God would come. They knew about it and desired that it would come, but they expected it to be a governmental change in the nation to free Israel from their Roman oppressors, something that the whole world would be able to see and witness. Jesus knows this and perhaps surprises or disappoints them by saying they will not be able to see it or observe it.

What does Jesus mean when he says it cannot be observed? If he said that the Kingdom is at hand, then surely we must be able to see it? If Jesus also said to be watchful of the signs (Matt. 24:42), how is it possible that it cannot be observed or seen? What is it exactly that we are to display in both powerful and majestic acts? The Greek word used is *paratereseos*, which means 'careful observation'. Therefore, the Kingdom of God does not come by careful observation alone. In other words, you cannot sit on your hands and do nothing, no matter how big they are! It does not happen through just observing, you have to be involved.

It is a spiritual Kingdom that will spread through those who follow Jesus. The Pharisees had not realised that the coming of the Kingdom had already begun. This is the Kingdom of God at hand, the first coming of Christ, not the second coming of Christ which is what will be clearly seen by this entire world (Matt. 24:30; Mark 13:26). Literally everyone can be involved, no matter your age or physical restriction, because it is a spiritual Kingdom, which advances through spiritual means. Prayer is an essential therefore, and all of us can pray! **We pray and then we obey**. In prayer, we hear God's voice and we do the practical things he asks of us. In this life, we will get the opportunity to reach those in the dominion of darkness and bring them into the Kingdom of Light.

Other translations say that the Kingdom *"is within you"* (ASV, TLB, NASB, NKJV), or *"within your grasp"* (ESV), or *"among you"* (NLT, Message, NRSV), or *"expanding in some of you"* (TPT). The Greek word is *entos* which means within, inside or among. So, the Kingdom is found within you – on the inside of you – and therefore is among us. Praise God!

When is this Kingdom?

The good news is that it is already here in our present time. As we have just seen, the Kingdom is at hand and is within us individually and among us as we gather together. It is in the here and now! That is why scriptures like in Matthew chapter sixteen can make sense… *"I tell you the truth, some who are standing here will not taste death before they see the Son of Man coming in his kingdom"* (Matt. 16:28). Jesus' ushering in of the Kingdom had begun. Jesus is in the middle of a discussion on discipleship when he promises that those living at the time would see Jesus coming in his Kingdom. This does not refer to or mean the second coming of Jesus, because we are still waiting for his return two-thousand years later, and those living back then certainly are not alive on earth today; they have tasted death. The promise was that they would see Jesus and how he really is in his Kingdom. Six days later came the transfiguration, when three of them did get a temporary and premature glimpse of Jesus in his glory (Matt. 17:1-2).

The Kingdom had been unleashed and the disciples got to see how glorious Jesus is, as the King of his Kingdom. As a disciple of Jesus today do you want to see the glory of Jesus now or are you waiting until you die to see his glory and majesty? I believe that in a vibrant and loving two-way relationship we can encounter him in many ways, just as we see in the scriptures. The Holy Spirit makes this type of encounter a very real possibility. If the disciples back then did not have to wait for this amazing experience, and encounter the glorified Jesus, then neither do we. The question is – are you actually seeking to encounter him? He may well surprise you and one day just show up. If he chooses to appear in the dreams of people of other faiths and people of no faith, then surely, he is able to show up for us too. God only gives us things that ultimately will benefit us and which we will call good (Luke 11:13). The promised Holy Spirit is good and has been given, and is continually given, that we might encounter both Jesus and the Father.

Whether you are in some form of education, or are perhaps unemployed, retired, working as a cleaner, nurse, teacher, scientist, engineer, small business owner or a corporate CEO, young or old – you have a sphere of influence i.e. circles within society in which you reside. In these, you can infuse the ways and principles of the Kingdom of Heaven into families, communities, institutions (including the Church!), schools, colleges, and clubs of every kind. Businesses can be run with the welfare of its staff as their highest priority, rather than purely for profit. People like Cadbury and Guinness started building businesses that transformed communities. They helped build housing, schools and hospitals for their entire workforce. Profit can be used to help others in many ways, and to help further Kingdom advancement.

Some places, particularly in the corporate world, may attempt to silence or forbid you from speaking about Jesus, wearing a cross, or praying for people. However, we can all humbly live out the spiritual fruit of the Kingdom, with things that cannot be prevented, namely, love, joy, peace, patience, kindness, goodness, faithfulness, gentleness and self-control (Gal. 5:22), in a Jesus servant-leadership style that applies honesty, mercy, wisdom and discernment. This applies when you are the boss and also when you're not! We can all be 'light' into dark places. Doing so will better help us to build bridges into the other kingdoms of this world, in this present age of the Kingdom, for Jesus.

The Kingdom to Come

Jesus will return physically to this earth, for his Bride the Church, and will establish his reign over this earth. We will see signs of this indicating it will soon take place… "*No-one knows about that day or hour, not even the angels in heaven, nor the Son, but only the Father*" (Matt. 24:36). So, we know that only the Father knows when all these things will happen. Mark puts it the same way, word for word in fact, but goes on to say… *"Be on guard! Be alert! You do not know when that time will come. It's like a man going away: he leaves his house and puts his servants in charge, each with his assigned task, and tells the one at the door to keep watch. Therefore keep watch because you do not know when the owner of the house will come back— whether in the evening, or at midnight, or when the cock crows, or at dawn. If he comes suddenly, do not let him find you sleeping. What I say to you, I say to everyone: 'Watch!'"* (Mark 13:33-37). We are to be watchful about signs in our present age, certainly, but they are not the overall focus.

One fairly recent example was seeing three blood-red moons in 2018, which was most likely a sign spoken about in the Book of Revelation, but only in part. In chapter six when the sixth seal is opened much more than a blood-red moon will appear (Rev. 6:12-17). Yet, the Christian media especially picked up on this and it was the talk of so many Christians. The sign had become the focus. For me, I would say that any sign should focus the believer's attention even more sharply on spreading the good news of the Kingdom. Which remember, is at hand. It is all around us and our message to others is to reach out and grab it.

Many have incorrectly prophesied when Jesus will return and many Christians spend much of their time focused on this subject of the end times. Unfortunately, this does not always turn into urgent action, but only more theorising and pontification. If we see signs that indicate Jesus might return, then they should push us to our main goal of extending the Kingdom in our spheres of influence.

The Kingdom is already here and we can encounter our King in the here and now of everyday life. We pray it into reality, in our lives and in the lives of those yet to discover Jesus. Yet, the Kingdom is still to come in its fullness. In the meantime, do not ignore or lose focus of the main thing, the big picture, the meta-narrative of the Biblical story: the union of heaven and earth, of God and people.

This 'present age' is ruled by Satan, but his power has been broken, with humanity now able to know and experience God's rule in their lives. Humanity does, however, remain free to reject the Kingdom. The 'age to come' begins with the *parousia* or the return of Jesus, the second coming of Christ. That day will come. Jesus will arrive in great victory, bringing his Kingdom in its fullness. He will establish his reign and remove all other kingdoms.

As this chapter closes, just think about the amazing position we find ourselves in, and what an incredible adventure our lives have been caught up into, and purposed for. The Kingdom is at hand and within us. We get to participate in extending it now, and living in it fully in the future. What greater call could there be on anyone's life?

CHAPTER FIVE

The Kingdom is not the Church

When we become a Christian and ask Jesus into our lives personally, we essentially give up our rights and privileges, in order to be obedient and also fruitful disciples. We choose to leave the kingdom of me, myself and I, and rather to **live under the Kingship of Jesus**. Life finds its true meaning in the hope that we have found and now wish to share with others. This does not mean we should stop our careers, quit our families and friendship groups, or no longer support Reading Football Club! Our focus of what is truly important simply changes.

We know that Jesus will one day return to this earth for his Bride, the Church, which we also become a part of when we actually enter the Kingdom. Yet the Kingdom retains a wider perspective, as we shall go on to see in the second section of this book. Often, we think that the Church and the Kingdom are names for the same thing. They are close relatives but they are not identical. I think it would help to bring greater clarity by looking at: 1) God's rule over his Kingdom, and 2) some of the differences between the Kingdom and the Church.

God's rule over his Kingdom

God has always ruled over his creation as seen in the Psalms (Psalm 9; 10; 24; 42; 86; 95; 96), and in the Prophets (Jer. 10:7, 10; 23:5-6; Isa. 6:5; 9:6-7; 43:15; Zech. 14:16). The concept of God ruling as a King over his creation is very present in the

OT, even if the same 'Kingdom of' terminology of the NT is not. Jesus however, broke into this world and ushered in a new and radically different Kingdom, creating (1 Cor. 11:25-26), and mediating (Heb. 8:6; 12:15) a new eternal (Heb. 13:20) covenant between God and humanity. The OT had seen God make three previous covenants or promises with mankind through Abraham, Moses and David. Jeremiah prophesied that a new covenant would come (Jer. 31:31-34).

Matthew's Gospel is full of such rich meaning and significance. It sits as the first book of the NT and, in its very first verse, introduces Jesus as the one who fulfils the covenant with Abraham to bless every nation, as well as the covenant with David that it will be everlasting. If that has left you wondering about the covenant with Moses (to provide a Kingdom of priests who minister to the world), well the structure of Matthew can be placed into five separate sections like the five books of Moses. After introductory chapters one-three, come chapters four to seven, eight to ten, eleven to thirteen, fourteen to twenty and then twenty-one to twenty-five, followed by concluding chapters twenty-six to twenty-eight. This structure alone would have been 'jaw-droppingly good', and 'sweet music to the ears' of those original Jewish Christian readers. They would have been wowed! Those entering the Kingdom become the priests who minister to this world.

From the point of the arrival of Jesus the Messiah and the announcement of his Kingdom, a very different type of Kingdom became available across this earth, one that mankind had not previously known. **It is an upside-down spiritual Kingdom of God's rule**, full of things like agape love, inner peace, and a power that can be demonstrated and displayed through its citizens.

The Greek word for kingdom *basileia* refers to the rank and authority of a king, who exercises authority over his realm or territory. The 'Kingdom of God' therefore refers to God's sovereignty and rule in action. God is actively involved in humanity to deliver it from bondage and sin, and we get to experience the reign of Jesus in the present, as we enter and live in his Kingdom.

As disciples, we do need to have both 'present' and 'future' viewpoints of the Kingdom. Otherwise, we would have to be content to live in it now, without a future hope of seeing the reality and fullness of it (only the present realm), or it would merely be a salvific insurance policy (only the future realm). The reason we desire heaven is because it is God's perfect reign, and that is what we aim for when we pray for the ways of heaven to materialise on earth. Without God reigning there, heaven would essentially be meaningless. So, we petition God to manifest his divine rule and power here, to push back the unrighteous kingdoms of this earth. Remember, the primary objective for disciples of Jesus is to know him by seeking first his Kingdom and his righteousness (Matt. 6:33).

The rest of the NT is littered with the theme of the Kingdom, with every epistle confirming this, as well as the Book of Acts beginning and ending with the Kingdom, and the Book of Revelation mentioning details of the future Kingdom. God is in charge and **we have the privilege of living under his rule, in his way, and for his purposes**.

Differences between Kingdom and Church

In the Gospel accounts, the actual word 'church' is mentioned only a few times (Matt. 16:18; 18:17), but 'kingdom' over one-hundred and twenty times, at least a 1:40 ratio, and yet, we seem to either perceive that they are synonymous or we tend to focus on the church. Why is this?

The main focus of Jesus was the teaching and demonstration of his Kingdom. This was to be the bedrock upon which the Church should then be built. The main focus of the NT outside of the Gospel accounts, is the formation of the Church from its beginnings at Pentecost, in the Book of Acts. However, within a generation, the various churches that had been formed, often began to struggle in one way or another. The Epistles focus on encouraging and also correcting churches' or individuals' thinking and behaviour. Jesus was fully aware who he would return for: his Bride the Church. His Kingdom teaching and demonstration was meant to be that steadying foundation on which everything else could fall back on, even the Church. We are absolutely indebted to the writing of those first Apostles, but sadly we still find both churches and individuals going somewhat astray today. We are still struggling with similar issues and should be learning from what these incredible people wrote. But what is our bedrock or our plumb-line? What should we fall back on? I believe that any church that focuses on the Kingdom guides people back to living like Jesus did, which will in turn help produce more effective churches, because we make more fruitful disciples. Jesus asked us to make disciples and leave the building of the Church to him, but how often do we attempt to swap these around? We do stand and applaud the likes of Paul, Peter and James; we learn from their adventures, sufferings, mistakes, victories and wisdom. They lived like Jesus. Yet there a missing focus that I feel is still occurring today, which is the need for a clearer understanding that enables disciples to live with a Kingdom perspective. This is the reason that this entire series focuses on the Gospel accounts and in particular, Matthew.

As time progressed through the centuries after the birth and formation of the Church, some great theologians came on the scene. They helped to define the things that we find difficult to understand. One of my favourites is Augustine of the sixth and seventh centuries, mainly because he first landed on the Isle of Thanet in 597AD, bringing Christianity to Britain. This is where I am privileged to live and minister. However, even great theologians are not perfect. Augustine was a Bishop sent from Rome, that had adopted Christianity as its state religion in the fourth century under Emperor Constantine. Augustine had been influenced by this fact and unhelpfully taught that the Kingdom was the visible, actual Church, thereby assimilating more power to the Church, that by this point in history had also merged with the political state. Therefore, we do need to better understand the relationship between the Kingdom and the Church, because they are not the same. By Church, I simply mean everyone who is a true disciple of Jesus, regardless of any individual church, para-church, organisation or ministry.

The Kingdom and the Church are inseparable, yet they have different identities. The Kingdom is God's rule, whereas the Church is a group of people who 'may' experience the Kingdom, and who at the same time, 'may' make up the community of the Kingdom. Take me as an example. For many years I was a born-again believer and follower of Jesus, but I was unclear about the Kingdom, my place in it, and that I was supposed to preach it. Yes, I did experience it on various occasions and often without realising, but I was in fact part of Christian communities that did not seem to have a clear focus on it. Note: this does not mean that God was not able to use my life during these times or that I was not saved, because he did and I was. These church communities were also Spirit filled.

Entrance to the Kingdom should lead to active participation in the Church, but entrance into a 'church membership' does not mean that a person has yet entered the Kingdom. We shall see later that the Kingdom includes both true and false disciples, but the 'true' Church can only include 'true' disciples. Church gatherings generally, of course, can include non-believers. They are supposed to be outposts of the wider Kingdom and will therefore attract both.

The Church's mission is to demonstrate the Kingdom in both words and power, meaning to share about Jesus and using spiritual gifts to demonstrate it. In other words, the Church is the instrument of the Kingdom. Jesus delegated his Kingdom authority to true disciples, who are now the custodians of the Kingdom, which somehow continues to grow and not diminish, even if our own church lacks revelation and understanding about the Kingdom. The Kingdom, however, advances through the power of the Holy Spirit and relies on his partnership. If individuals in the Church reject the Holy Spirit then the wider Church cannot be the same as the Kingdom.

The Church is created out of the Kingdom and is supposed to be the primary witness of the Kingdom to this world, but God can also work in miraculous ways outside of the Church. While he will and frequently does use Christians to do his bidding, God is not limited to, or dependent upon, our obedience, and works in the hearts of people who do not yet know him, in places that we may never see. Let me help put this into some context. Missiology, the theory and study of mission, indicates that throughout history only a maximum one-third of the world population have been followers of Jesus, at any one time. In other words, there has always been a target audience of two-thirds of the world. The Church does reach into much of the world, whereas the Kingdom covers the entire world.

Finally, the Kingdom is eternal, whilst the Church has a time and place in history, i.e. the time between the ascension of Jesus and his return to this earth. We will end up in the future eternal Kingdom, not in a church. I am by no means belittling the incredible Church, all the amazing things that she has done and continues to do, in so many places since she was first formed. I love the Church and will always be faithful to her, as the primary instrument to make disciples and extend the influence of the Kingdom.

CHAPTER SIX

The Kingdom of Heaven in Matthew's Gospel

Matthew wrote his Gospel to the Jewish Christian community, to teach them that Jesus was the Messiah and the one who fulfilled the Jewish laws in the Torah, as well as the writings of the Prophets. Matthew wants them to know how to now live, in light of the fact that God's Son had walked this earth and ushered in a new Kingdom. These newly converted Christians would then know how they were supposed to act and behave in this Kingdom, and to be truer witnesses of it, as they took its message to Israel and then to the rest of the world. The 'Kingdom of Heaven' is Matthew's major theme and is mentioned over thirty times. The reason Matthew uses this term rather than 'Kingdom of God', is because in Jewish culture they did not dare to use God's actual name, out of fear and reverence of God's utter holiness, and so the phrase used is a suitable substitute for that divine name.

Switching back now to the OT momentarily, in the Book of Deuteronomy, the ten commandments are given (Deut. 5:6-21). These laws were meant to be a directive, but also a joyous heartfelt response out of one's love for God, so much so, that they consume a person. They become all that we talk about. We see this in chapter six... *"Hear, O Israel: The Lord our God, the Lord is one. Love the Lord your God with all your heart and with all your soul and with all your strength. These commandments* that I give you today are to be **upon your hearts. Impress them on your children. Talk about them when you sit at home and when you walk along the road, when you lie down and when you get up**" (Deut. 6:4-7).

Matthew uses the text from Deuteronomy that Jesus quoted, to sum up, and enhance the OT law... *"Jesus replied: "'Love the Lord your God with all your heart and with all your soul and with all your mind.' This is the first and greatest commandment. And the second is like it: 'Love your neighbour as yourself.' All the Law and the Prophets hang on these two commandments""* (Matt. 22:37-40).

This text would have been known to the Jewish Christian audience, who would have immediately recognised and identified with Moses' teaching. Jesus makes religious laws into a relational option once again. Remember that Israel had rejected a face-to-face relationship with God as they wanted a representative, i.e. Moses, to speak to God on their behalf, which necessitated living with the laws God gave to Moses.

In this new Kingdom of Heaven, its citizens, both back in the first century and today, are to love God with every part of their being. Jesus adds soul and mind into the equation leaving no doubt that he means he wants all of you. Once this relationship is restored 'upwardly' to God the Father then you will be able to 'outwardly' love your neighbour and 'inwardly' love yourself. A cord of three strands is not quickly broken (Ecc. 4:12). If we work on these first as the greatest commandments, we will be able to fix much that is currently broken in the

Church today, like our behaviour! If any Church has lost focus, it can always fall back upon the Kingdom to refocus once more.

This book, and the future ones in this series, will therefore predominately focus on Matthew's Gospel and the 'Kingdom of Heaven' it teaches. It is Matthew who uniquely uses this exquisite phase.

Try looking at Matthew's first themes from the mindset of first-century Jewish converts to Christianity, who were by this time expecting or already experiencing persecution and perhaps they were becoming unsure of their new faith in Jesus...

Chapter 1
- The Genealogies from Abraham.
- The virgin birth of Jesus.

Chapter 2
- The Magi worship Jesus at his birthplace.
- The family escape to Egypt.
- The return to Nazareth.

Chapter 3
- John the Baptist prepares the way for Jesus.
- Jesus' Baptism – a trinitarian moment.

Chapter 4
- Jesus tested in the wilderness.
- Jesus begins to preach.
- Jesus calls the disciples.
- Jesus begins to heal the sick.

Chapters 5, 6 & 7
- Jesus turns the existing laws upside down.

I think that reading just this far in Matthew for the first time would have meant so much to its original readers and completely reaffirmed their faith.

As disciples of Jesus today: 1) we are people of God on mission with God (territory), 2) we live an adventurous life, with expectation for now and with real anticipation for the future (citizens), 3) we know the King's heart and obey his will (laws), and 4) we cannot be separated from Jesus (King).

We find all four Kingdom components within this unique 'Kingdom of Heaven' Gospel.

CHAPTER SEVEN

Responses to the Kingdom of Heaven

I gave my life to Jesus at the age of twenty-one and within a couple of years had started to learn to play the guitar. This was so that I could simply worship at home whenever I wanted, and give my worship to God in the secret place, where I could play and sing with little skill and no embarrassment! Of course, over time, I was able to improve and ended up on the church worship team. I would occasionally lead worship in smaller midweek groups and would attend as many conferences on worship leading and song writing that I could, so that I could progress and one day become a 'real' worship leader. However, the issue I faced at the time was one of an unhealthy comparison to nationally and internationally known worship leaders. I had heard them teach and had seen their greater musicianship and skills in singing. For me, it was less a case of idolising and longing to be like them, but rather that I could never be as good. I lacked confidence. I was not very good and would never be able to be 'great' at it. This perception held me back from serving God in his church with the freedom and joy that I had back in the secret place. Comparison should be healthy to help one aspire to achieve something, but for me it was negatively unhealthy and was not at all helpful. Hold that thought! I will come back to this story in a few pages, to show its relevance.

As we continue through Matthew, we see…

Chapters 8 & 9
- Jesus demonstrates the Kingdom further.

Chapter 10
- Disciples are authorised to demonstrate it.
- Discipleship requires our total commitment.
- Disciples should expect opposition.
- Discipleship requires ultimate loyalty to Jesus.

Chapter 11
- Discipleship means Seeking the Father.

Chapter 12
- Jesus as Lord of the Sabbath and head of the Kingdom.

The Parable of the Sower

As we reach chapter thirteen, we see that it contains many parables describing what **the Kingdom of Heaven is like**…but the important 'Parable of the Sower' comes first to give us some solid grounding.

Matthew goes to great lengths to explain about the sower using twenty-three verses (Matt. 13:1-23), Mark uses eighteen verses (Mark 4:3-20), Luke uses twelve verses (Luke 8:4-15); with John not mentioning it at all. This familiar parable is well worth another read at this point, if you would like to use these references.

In verses one through nine, Matthew informs us that the Parable of the Sower was told to the crowd that had gathered around Jesus. In this parable, Jesus tells a story of someone who sows seeds on four different types of ground. The first, was a hard path and the seed could not grow and was instantly snatched up. The second, was on rocky ground and the seed was able to begin growing, but could not grow deep roots and so it withered in the sun. The third, was on thorny ground and the seed could grow, but it could not compete with the number of thorns around it. The fourth, was on good soil that allowed the seed to plant deep, grow strong and produce fruit.

In verses ten through seventeen Matthew explains the reason Jesus gave for speaking in parables, because… *"**the knowledge of the secrets** of the kingdom of heaven **has been given to you, but not to them**"*. Matthew uses seven verses to do so, Mark explains this in four verses and Luke only uses two. Again, why does Matthew go the extra mile here? Perhaps he additionally quoted Isaiah from the OT because he wrote predominately to a Jewish audience, and he uses this fact to drive home that Jesus is the Messiah, who teaches in the way that Isaiah foretold.

As Matthew begins to unpack the meaning of the parable in verses eighteen to twenty-three, he recalls Jesus' words… *"when anyone hears the message **about the kingdom**"*, to reiterate that his parable is most certainly about the Kingdom. Jesus uses this parable to explain that there are four different responses to the good news of his Kingdom.

On the hard path: describes the ones who hear and do not understand, and the evil one comes and snatches away what was sown in their heart [Luke adds *'so that they may not believe and be saved'*]. This hard ground or path represents someone with a **hard heart** that hears the word of God but does not accept it. Satan can steal from this person meaning there is no growth at all.

On rocky ground: refers to someone who hears the word and at once receives it with joy. But since they have no root, they last only a short time [Luke says *'they believe for a while'*]. When trouble or persecution comes [Luke says *'in times of testing'*] because of the word, they quickly fall away. This stony or rocky ground is someone who shows interest in the gospel but who has an **unconvinced heart**; because when trouble comes their faith is not strong enough to stand.

Among the thorns: refers to someone who hears the word, but the worries of this life and the deceitfulness of wealth choke the word [Mark adds *'and the desires for other things come in'*], making it unfruitful [Luke adds *'they are choked by life's worries, riches and pleasures, and they do not mature'*]. This thorny ground is a person who receives the gospel but who has many other idols and distractions in life, a **divided heart** which stunts growth.

On good soil: refers to someone [Luke adds *'those with a noble and good heart'*] who hears the word and understands it [Mark adds *'accepts it'*]. *"This is the one who produces a crop, yielding a hundred, sixty or thirty times what was sown"*. The good soil is someone who has heard and received or accepted the word of God and allows it to take root and grow within their life – a **noble and humble heart**.

Most would say that the sower is Jesus and the seed is the word of God. Perhaps there is nothing new there for you, as this is a passage often preached. However, I would want to add, that as disciples of Jesus today we are supposed to **keep on sowing**. Paul says, *"I planted the seed, Apollos watered it, but God has* *been making it grow…For we are co-workers in God's service"* (1 Cor. 3:6, 9a). Matthew's Gospel also ends by telling us that we must keep on making disciples (Matt. 28:18-20) – this means that we must keep on sowing.

Therefore, knowing the responses to our ongoing sowing is really helpful, so that we can be equipped and understand what is most likely taking place. This wisdom enables us to see what is happening in people, rather than becoming despondent or worse giving up, through a lack of awareness.

Unhealthy Comparison

Going back to the point of sharing my story of unhealthy comparisons: some would look at this parable and compare their own lives to it. Which one are they? Which one might you be?

1) I feel like I'm not worthy to approach God or come to church or to take communion (I must be like the seed on the hard path).
2) I feel like I'm locked into bad choices and sin that I cannot escape from so I'm not worthy (I must be like the seed on rocky ground).
3) I feel like I'm pulled by material things and I tend to worry a lot so I'm not worthy (I must be like the seed among thorns).
4) I'm seeing fruit in me and around me so I am certainly worthy now to approach God (I must be like the seed on good soil).

This type of comparison is not always helpful as it is usually a negative one for the first three, or it is sometimes 'proudly' positive for the fourth. This can lead to even becoming judgemental of others if they're not in the good soil... *"For by the grace given me I say to every one of you: Do not think of yourself more highly than you ought, but rather think of yourself with sober judgment"* (Rom. 12:3). Notice how this comes right after the famous scripture about being transformed by the renewing of your mind (Rom. 12:1-2). Renewing your mind will help both the negative and positive thinking towards this parable, and give us a healthier balance.

In or Out the Kingdom

In the USA, well certainly in Texas, there is a fast-food chain called In-N-Out Burger. Seeing it, ok I confess I was actually enjoying eating a burger there, reminded me of being in or out of the Kingdom, not the burger! Some that follow Jesus today still compartmentalise their lives, so much so that they behave one way with their work colleagues and completely differently when around church folk. We cannot be in and out of the Kingdom. If we are in then we must learn to live like it, in every area of our lives. We must learn not to compartmentalise life and behave in ways that are acceptable to others, but that do not reflect the Kingdom.

We are either in the Kingdom of light or we are still in the Kingdom of darkness. Which is it? Paul says... *"giving thanks to the Father, who **has qualified you** to share in the inheritance of the saints [or his holy people] in the kingdom of light. For **he has rescued us** from the dominion of darkness and brought us into the kingdom of the Son he loves"* (Col. 1:12-13).

Therefore, as disciples of Jesus and those who are born again, we are in his Kingdom. God himself has qualified you! Our rightful governmental position before God and our new identity is certainly in the Kingdom of Heaven, even if we still sometimes act to the contrary. We are saints or holy people (justification) that sometimes sin, though hopefully less and less so as we progress through life as a disciple (sanctification). If we mess up, and we all do, the text does not say that we hop back into the kingdom of darkness.

We either have our names written in the Lamb's Book of Life or we don't... *"Nothing impure will ever enter it [the new Jerusalem], nor will anyone who does what is shameful or deceitful,* but **only those whose names are written in the Lamb's book of life**" (Rev. 21:27). If we are in the Kingdom then our name is also therefore written into the Lamb's Book of Life. This is great news!

When we do go wrong as disciples, I believe that what is at stake is our effectiveness for the King and our intimacy with him. I do not believe that because of our mistakes, even if they happen frequently, God rubs out our name from this book, nor does he switch our kingdom allegiance depending upon our behaviour. Yes, of course, our behaviour may affect how close we seem to feel towards God, but that is an emotional response. How I feel is not always in right alignment with what the truth of scripture says about me. God says that he will never leave us or forsake us (Josh. 1:5; Heb. 13:5). This is part of the lifelong sanctification process of growing closer to God and living holier lives, all of which is temporary anyway.

Why this Parable?

I do not personally think that this parable was meant to make us stumble in the sanctification process. Rather we should view it in light of the bigger picture of God's Kingdom and the fact that we are justified before God because of the sacrifice of Jesus – which is eternal. We need to see the meta-narrative of Christianity and seek the glory of heaven to fall on earth. For it to be demonstrated through us as broken vessels, into a broken and hurting world. I believe that Jesus gave us the Parable of the Sower, to teach us how important the state of the 'human heart' is to receiving his gospel, and to explain that upfront, so that we will not become discouraged as we sow these same seeds two-thousand years later. We all want to be good soil disciples and the truth of scripture points to this being the case, even though we mess things up, make poor choices and sin. These things do not put us in the first three categories of the parable. We must stop comparing ourselves! We are good soil disciples with God still pruning us.

Knowing how those in the Kingdom of darkness will respond to the Kingdom of Heaven is what this parable is about. After all, it was only a few chapters earlier, in chapter ten, that Jesus had sent out the first disciples on their own. This helps us now to be forewarned and armed, so that the responses that we get will not discourage us as we keep sowing today. With this important grounding in the types of responses we will see, now in place, Jesus goes on to describe what the Kingdom of Heaven is actually like.

The Kingdom of Heaven is like...

CHAPTER ONE

Wheat and Weeds

The 'Kingdom of Heaven is like' references are given in parables, and are pieces of a jigsaw that we will be putting together over the coming chapters. But first, here are a few thoughts on gardening.

For me, like many others, life has been busy and the gardening was always just another chore. I would rush through it as fast as I could so it would at least be a pleasant space. I had discovered moments of solitude in the garden and at times found it therapeutic to plant and dig and cut stuff. Please excuse me if you are a keen gardener and know the Latin names of everything green. However, I have never been taught (or tried to learn) the ins and outs of gardening and so I probably spent a lot of time pulling up the wrong things and killing off the right things! Cutting something that should be left to grow and planting things at the wrong time of year. But we all know of the endless frustration of weeds. It seems no matter how much careful digging and pulling up we do, and no matter how much weed killer we put down, they just keep coming back. In the parable of the wheat and weeds (or tares) we see the age-old problem of those pesky weeds!

The introductory parable of the sower had a break in between the parable itself (Matt. 13:3-9) and its given definition or meaning (Matt. 13:18-23). Likewise, this first parable describing what the Kingdom of Heaven is like, called the 'wheat and weeds', has the parable (Matt. 13:24-30) and then an interlude of other parables, before the meaning is given (Matt. 13:36-43). This is a parable about the Kingdom not about the Church, as I shall explain later.

The Parable of Wheat and Weeds

*"Jesus told them another parable: "The kingdom of heaven is like a man who sowed good seed in his field. 25 But **while everyone was sleeping**, his enemy came and sowed weeds among the wheat, and went away. 26 When the wheat sprouted and formed ears, then the weeds also appeared. 27 The owner's servants came to him and said, 'Sir, didn't you sow good seed in your field? Where then did the weeds come from?' 28 'An enemy did this,' he replied. The servants asked him, 'Do you want us to go and pull them up?' 29 'No,' he answered, 'because while you are pulling the weeds, you may root up the wheat with them. 30 Let both grow together until the harvest. At that time I will tell the harvesters: First collect the weeds and tie them in bundles to be burned; then gather the wheat and bring it into my barn"'"* (Matt. 13:24-30).

A man sows good seed in his field and when everyone is asleep, the enemy comes and sows weeds into the same place that the good seeds have been sown. The first thing to learn is that we as disciples need to be spiritually disciplined, staying spiritually alert by keeping watch, through prayer. When we are 'sleeping' or unaware, the enemy comes in to do his mischief, to disrupt the good work of sowing good seeds that we are attempting to do today. Peter tells us this as well… *"be self-controlled [of sober mind] and alert. Your enemy the devil prowls around like a roaring lion looking for someone to devour"* (1 Peter 5:8).

As the wheat now begins to grow and break through the surface, right behind and alongside come the weeds (tares) that have also been sown. A tare is thought to be something called darnel which is typically known as either darnel, poison darnel or darnel ryegrass. Its full name is *Lolium Temulentum*. Interestingly darnel is found in widespread locations all over this **world**.

As darnel begins to grow it looks very similar to wheat, in fact, you can hardly tell the difference between them in their infancy. It is only when they are mature that it becomes easier to tell them apart. Is this perhaps the reality of our lives as disciples walking with God, that we are still so similar in behaviour to those who don't follow Jesus that we can barely be found apart? We are supposed to be holy *hagios* which means to be set apart for God, to be sacred, to be different. Our lives of purity and holiness should stand us out from the crowd, in a good and positive way.

As the wheat and weeds mature, you will more clearly be able to see the difference. In some way, we all began as weeds or tares, until we entered the Kingdom. Immediately after entering the Kingdom our lives often remain much the same as before we were saved – unless we had a dramatic conversion like Paul on the road to Damascus. It is usually only after some time and growing as disciples that our lives will be differentiated from those not yet in the Kingdom. Even the apostle Paul had to spend some time apart in Tarsus to grow in God (Acts 9:30), before Barnabas later went to find him (Acts 11:25) and encourage him into a life of mission. Entering the Kingdom does not suddenly make us perfect.

Darnel has a stronger root system than wheat and…
- Negatively impacts agriculture
- Negatively impacts human health
- Negatively impacts animal health

How is this possible? Well darnel is poisonous, which means that it is definitely not good for us. When people eat its seeds, they can get dizzy, become off-balance and even nauseous. Apparently, its official name comes from a Latin word for drunk.

Back to the text…the servants are the first ones to recognise that the soil has produced some destructive weeds. They want to understand what went wrong – how could this have possibly happened. They want to identify and remove them.

The owner recognises this as a work of the enemy but also knows that removing the weeds with a stronger root system will cause damage to the wheat. Also, as they look very similar to the wheat in the early stages the wheat could easily get removed by mistake.

Both the servants and the owner recognise things quickly, but do we even recognise that we are in a spiritual battle for a spiritual Kingdom against a spiritual enemy? We simply have to be an alert people, who pray both individually and together as the gathered church. We simply must be passionate about prayer, which should be something so very natural to us. Why then, is the church prayer meeting often not well attended or vibrant? It can be difficult to develop a praying church but it shouldn't be so. That is an oxymoron for me. If we understand that our purpose in prayer is to uproot demonic structures, that will bring freedom into people's lives, then we can realise or actualise the rending of heaven to help bring change to this earth. To be able to do this, we must be able to **recognise**, **remove** and know how to **restrict** the enemy's influence upon us as individuals. This will further enable our lives, and our prayers, to uproot negative and demonic influences in the spiritual realm, wherever we go.

God sees all things and knows that evil exists alongside good. He allows this because he wants all people to willingly turn to him. The owner tells the servants to wait until maturity and then to harvest the whole field, in order to save the wheat. It will then be easier to distinguish – one for keeping and one for throwing away. A day of reckoning will come! The big picture or the meta-narrative of the Bible is that all will face this day of reckoning. The point of this is not that we relish the fact that we are in the Kingdom and will spend eternity in paradise; not that we think lightly of our reckoning because of Jesus' sacrifice on our behalf; not that we recognise we live in a world of good and evil; but rather that we see the urgency of telling non-believers about the Kingdom we have entered… *"For you have been born again, not of perishable seed, but of imperishable, through the living and enduring word of God"* (1 Peter 1:23).

The Meaning

"Then he left the crowd and went into the house. His disciples came to him and said, "Explain to us the parable of the weeds in the field." [37] *He answered, "The **one who sowed** the good seed is the <u>Son of Man</u>.* [38] ***The field** is the <u>world</u>, and the **good seed** stands for the <u>people of the kingdom</u>. The **weeds** are the <u>people</u>*

of the evil one, ³⁹ *and* **the enemy** *who sows them is the* <u>devil</u>. **The harvest** *is the* <u>end of the age</u>, *and the* **harvesters** *are* <u>angels</u>. ⁴⁰ *"As the weeds are pulled up and burned in the fire, so it will be at the end of the age.* ⁴¹ *The Son of Man will send out his angels, and they will weed out of his kingdom everything that causes sin and all who do evil.* ⁴² *They will throw them into the blazing furnace, where there will be weeping and gnashing of teeth.* ⁴³ *Then the righteous will shine like the sun in the kingdom of their Father. Whoever has ears, let them hear""* (Matt. 13:36-43).

Jesus leaves the boat from which he has been teaching the crowds and now goes into the more private setting of a house with his disciples. Interestingly they ask him about this parable and not the other parables of the 'mustard seed' and the 'yeast' (Matt. 13:31-35). Perhaps they could see it held more wide-ranging ramifications for all mankind, when compared to the others.

The Sower is Jesus, 'the Son of Man' being the same term that Daniel used to refer to Jesus, when Jesus was first handed the Kingdom. Today, we are to continue sowing for Jesus.

The Field is the world NOT the Church. Some try to use this parable to illustrate true and false prophets in the Church. However, Jesus was not talking about the mixed character or nature of the Church. **The territory of the Kingdom is this entire world**. We are to be witnesses of the Kingdom and demonstrate it in both **word** and **power** – to Jerusalem, Judea, Samaria and to the ends of the earth (Acts 1:8).

The Good Seed are those in the Kingdom. Notice that in the 'parable of the sower' seed means the word of God, but here in the 'parable of the wheat and weeds', seed is the result of what was sown i.e. people now in the Kingdom.

The Weeds are those not yet in the Kingdom and following Satan, even if they are unaware that is what they are doing. 'Everybody welcome nobody judged' is a key statement for my church. What we simply mean by it is that we allow those who don't know Jesus into our midst without judging them. They will recognise it immediately if they are judged. We want them to feel like they belong, so that they can encounter Jesus personally, that means through our lives too, which are supposed to reflect Jesus. "I once was lost but now I'm found", as the old hymn goes. We have to always remember where we came from and the amazing grace God has shown to us!

The Enemy is the Devil. That is clear. We have a spiritual enemy sowing in the same territory as us, but for evil. The Devil does try to destroy Christ's work through false believers found in the Church, but he also does this through teachers in secular settings as well, i.e. the world outside of the Church, who also lead many astray.

The Harvest is the end of the world. This is when Jesus returns and sorts things out! It will be easy for Jesus to tell apart those who belong in his Kingdom.

The Harvesters are angels. Those who are sent to do the sorting of those in and those not in the Kingdom. All people have been living in the same territory of the Kingdom or rule of God, i.e. this world, but many have not acknowledged Jesus as the King. Let's be clear, there will be one coming judgement and as part of that, the angels pull out of the Kingdom all that have not been made right with the Father, through Jesus his Son.

In Conclusion

Jesus warns his disciples to live by this parable… *"if you have ears to hear"*. In other words, please pay attention! The Kingdom is everywhere, right across this planet. There can be those around us not yet part of the Kingdom, 'pretenders' in our church environments, or even spies in the camp who have their own agendas. The Kingdom has invaded human history without disrupting the other kingdoms of this world and their various societal structures. God does permit other kingdoms to exist, like the kingdom of me, myself and I, as well as various ungodly worldviews and societal structures, the beauty of this natural world and all its wealth, and the kingdom of evil or darkness. It was these very kingdoms that Satan used to tempt Jesus with (Matt. 4:8-10). Therefore, the enemy does have an influence in the wider territory of the Kingdom of Heaven, blinding many people to the gospel. If Satan was able to tempt Jesus, then he is still able to tempt us, to oppress us and to negatively influence those who are in the Kingdom of Heaven – if we let him!

The bigger picture of the Kingdom of Heaven shows that disciples or called out ones, i.e. the Church, will always live alongside an ungodly culture or society. Yet in his mercy God allows both the wheat and the weeds to co-exist side by side and the ability for one to influence the other… *"He causes his sun to rise on the evil and the good, and sends rain on the righteous and the unrighteous"* (Matt. 5:45). When the Kingdom of Heaven comes to its fruition there will no longer be 'weeds' among the 'wheat'. For now, though, God permits both good and evil to continue to develop and mature side by side in this world.

We are not the gatekeepers of the Kingdom of Heaven, choosing who is in and who is not, as we too will face judgement – thank you, Papa, for sending Jesus – because as disciples of Jesus, we will be declared not guilty, because of the work of the cross.

This parable too is about the sowing of seeds. It brings us to a sobering conclusion about the Kingdom, and that by God's grace we find ourselves part of it. This should motivate us to carry out the great commission, taking the message of the Kingdom of Heaven to the ends of the earth, in both word and powerful demonstration. Briggs puts it this way… *"You have been summoned to deliberate, legislate and exert the will of God against demonic systems, injustice and false ideologies. Ekklesia, remember who you are".*[9] We the *ekklesia*, or the 'called out' ones, are to live sacrificial lives of repentance, continually turning towards God. This will require discipline and tenacity, but also moving in the power of the Holy Spirit to take dominion to extend the Kingdom of Heaven. When the Church engages in local evangelism and mission, we are able

---

[9] Briggs, D. *Ekklesia Rising. The Authority of Christ in Communities of Contending Prayer* (Kansas: Champion Press, 2014).

to sow many more seeds than when we sit inside our buildings, which is where the enemy wants to keep us.

CHAPTER TWO

Mustard Seed

Next come two much shorter parables: firstly the 'mustard seed' and secondly the 'yeast' or leaven (Matt. 13:31-35). Both of these seem to have the same point in mind which is the **growth** of the Kingdom.

I thought it would be helpful as we look at the 'mustard seed' to venture outside of Matthew and lean on both Mark and Luke to help us expand our understanding of what Jesus is teaching us.

The Mustard Seed

Matthew… *"He told them another parable: "The kingdom of heaven is like a mustard seed, which a man took and **planted in his field**. ³² Though it is the **smallest of all seeds**, yet when it grows, it is the **largest of garden plants** and becomes a tree, so that the birds of the air come and **perch in its branches**""* (Matt. 13:31-32).

Mark… *"Again he said, "What shall we say the kingdom of God is like, or what parable shall we use to describe it? ³¹ It is like a mustard seed, which is the **smallest of all seed you plant in the ground**. ³² Yet when planted, it grows and becomes the **largest of all garden plants**, with such big branches that the birds of the air can **perch in its shade**""* (Mark 4:30-32).

Luke... *"Then Jesus asked, "What is the kingdom of God like? What shall I compare it to? ¹⁹ It is like a mustard seed, which a man took and **planted in his garden**. It grew and became a tree, and the birds of the air **perched in its branches**""* (Luke 13:18-19).

The mustard seed was the smallest herb seed, commonly planted in the region of the world in which Jesus lived and ministered. The point was not to state scientifically that no other seeds exist in the world that could potentially be smaller, but rather Jesus wanted to use an illustration that everyone would understand. There are smaller seeds in existence like the orchid flower which grows in tropical rainforest environments, but as an agrarian or farming society, the original hearers would all have completely understood the meaning of a mustard seed, as something with a very small beginning and the comparison to how large the end result would be. Therefore, it is certainly a Kingdom that shall experience **powerful growth**.

The plant referred to here is generally considered to be black mustard, a large plant that grows each year up to nine feet (2.7m) tall. The Jewish community did not grow the plant in their gardens, which is therefore consistent with how Matthew described it as growing in a field. Luke tells the parable with the plant in a generic garden instead, so that his original hearers outside of Israel would better understand. Mark doesn't say where it is planted. Once sown it is nearly impossible to get the area free from it, as the seed germinates so quickly when it falls.

The mustard seed is about 1/25th of an inch (1mm) in size and takes around ten days to germinate. This means that it begins to grow and put out shoots after a short period of dormancy. Wouldn't it be easy if we just had to wait for ten days to see new life springing up and the Kingdom being added to? If that were the case and our personal experience, we wouldn't ever grow in the spiritual fruit of patience, yet globally this does take place. But let also me remind you that it was a ten-day prayer meeting in the upper room before Pentecost sprung up out of the ground! I'm sure the disciples must have gotten rather disappointed at times and wondered how they, by following this homeless carpenter, could change anything, let alone the world.

Regarding this particular parable, Witherington helpfully comments that... "*Though the dominion appeared small like a seed during Jesus' ministry, it would inexorably grow into something large and firmly rooted, which some would find shelter in and others would find obnoxious and try to root out*".[10] The significance of the nesting birds is perhaps that people will find a place of rest, protection and spiritual sustenance in the Kingdom.

In Conclusion

We must never despise small beginnings. Whether that is in your own life, in your career, in your church, or your ministry. We can of course at times feel insignificant or small or

---

[10] Witherington, B. *The Gospel of Luke* (Cambridge: Cambridge University Press, 2018).

unimportant. This parable helps us to see things in a different light if we can patiently follow God's ways. If we keep on knowing and serving God, then the seeds we sow will begin to take root. It might be a while before we see things above ground, or in the natural realm, and that's normal for most of us. But we must be expectant to see powerful growth.

The Kingdom has been planted now in an unexpected way, but planted none the less. It started with just a few, and so it has seen powerful growth up until today. Even if it does still seem small wherever you happen to be, remember that it grows, and that the final outcome of the Kingdom in its fullness is inevitable, now that the process of growth has begun.

CHAPTER THREE

Yeast

The parable of the 'yeast' is also referring to growth, so I expect that growth was important to Jesus.

But first, a confession. Like gardening my cooking skills are also not that great. Some of you are cooking experts and make incredible food, even winning cooking competitions. I did manage this once, but by cheating and entering a caterpillar cake mix as 'little Johnny' into the children's category, at one of our church bake-off competitions. Whilst I got away with it and wasn't spotted, I did later confess to all! Moving quickly back onto the parable of the yeast...

The Yeast
"He told them still another parable: "The kingdom of heaven is like yeast that a woman took and mixed into a large amount [about sixty pounds] of flour until it worked all through the dough"" (Matt. 13:33).

Leaven or yeast is a fungus that bakers have used to make bread for thousands of years. When yeast (old fermented dough) is added to a large quantity of flour, the newly made dough swallows up or seemingly consumes the yeast, so that it is almost unnoticeable. Yet, the living organisms in the yeast grow rapidly overnight, so that by morning the entire quantity of dough has been affected. The yeast causes fermentation, which is a chemical breakdown of the material. This produces noticeable results: the bread rises.

Similarly, the Kingdom of Heaven came through someone who was put to death and left only a handful of disciples. But do not let this deceive you, they had life to give, which meant that something far grander was on its way!

In the five books attributed to Moses, there are over thirty references to not using yeast in various religious practices. Unleavened bread is bread that is made without leaven or yeast. Without yeast, bread is unleavened and it remains flat and dense. The Israelites ate unleavened bread as part of the Passover celebration. It was symbolic of the haste with which the Israelites fled Egypt during the Exodus – they left so quickly that the bread did not have time to rise. God instructed them to commemorate the event by eating unleavened bread... *"You shall eat no leavened bread with it. Seven days you shall eat it with unleavened bread, the bread of affliction—for you came out of the land of Egypt in haste—that all the days of your life you may remember the day when you came out of the land of Egypt"* (Deut. 16:3). For the preparation of the Passover, leaven was not to be found in the house, because it could act as a contaminant. Interestingly, in Leviticus, there are two exceptions to this, when yeast was in fact prescribed (Lev. 7:13; 23:17).

The amount used, sixty pounds, holds significance because it equates to three measures, which is the amount used by Sarah to bake bread when she and Abraham were visited by the angels (Gen. 18:6). It is also the amount used for baking the shewbread in the Tabernacle of the Lord (Lev. 24:5).

Yeast symbolises influence and is usually found to be the negative sort. Just as a little bit of yeast works through and permeates all the dough, and so does influence, be it good or bad. Paul likens yeast to **false teaching** (Gal. 5:9). A little sin will affect an entire church, nation, or the whole of a person's life. Sin starts in thought, which then affects the will and the actions, leading eventually to spiritual death (James. 1:14-15). Other negative connotations appear in the Synoptic Gospels where Jesus warns to beware of the yeast of the Pharisees, which is likened to **hypocrisy**. Paul also uses yeast as a metaphor for **boasting** (1 Cor. 5:6-8). He instructs us to get rid of bread with old yeast (removal of sin or a corrupting influence) and to use new bread without yeast which represents holiness.

Once dough has been leavened it is impossible to cleanse out the yeast, because it has permeated right through it. Can you see the destructive influence that sin has? We simply cannot remove it no matter how much we try. Wonderfully though, Jesus' sacrifice on the cross paid for our sin making it possible for us be made holy, to be made clean… "*If we confess our sins, he is faithful and just and will forgive us our sins and purify [to cleanse] us from all unrighteousness*" (1 John 1:9).

In seemingly the only positive usage of yeast in the Bible, Jesus says that the Kingdom of Heaven is actually like yeast. Jesus uses yeast to describe the positive impact and powerful influence associated with his Kingdom. He is the bread of life after all (John 6:35).

In Conclusion

Some would view these last two parables of the mustard seed and now the yeast, from a negative standpoint of evil, because the nesting birds from the 'mustard seed' they interpret as unbelievers, and 'yeast' or leaven is portrayed as the spread of evil. However, scripturally we can see in other places the same symbol used for both evil and good. For example, the Lion represents Satan prowling around and also Jesus as the Lion of the tribe of Judah. Therefore, the mustard seed and birds nesting, along with the yeast, can also be seen as positive and good symbols.

I believe both parables are being used to describe the Kingdom of Heaven – which is very good. The power of this Kingdom influences and transforms individual lives for the better, who in turn can spread that same influence and growth to others. It's called making disciples!

If we only look at the natural realm in front of us, we can quite easily become discouraged and disappointed. So, we must also be looking, in the spiritual realm, to see growth in people, whilst not losing sight of the ultimate destiny of this incredible Kingdom, of which we are a part. We should remain full of hope and optimism because we know what is really happening, the very real influence of the Kingdom, is permeating the world through 'little old' you and me.

CHAPTER FOUR

Hidden Treasure

If you could have anything that you would want – what would you choose, what would you ask for?

In first world countries we would probably ask for a nice house, a great car, the most amazing job with a huge salary, a wonderful family – or perhaps all of these things. But think for a moment…what is the largest ancient treasure chest, room or palace, filled with the most precious gold and jewels, that you could possibly imagine! Wouldn't it be great to be that rich so that we could, of course, bless others…but more likely to ensure that we and our closest have every luxury that this world can offer?

However, in the third world, the list might look a little different: enough food not to starve, a small dwelling with some warmth and no leaking roof, not having to beg or no longer having to sell yourself. The difference of realities is a stark one.

Perhaps some on this planet, hopefully including us, would seek something more noble like happiness and fulfilment, or perhaps love and justice. Would any be bold like Solomon and ask for wisdom?

Here we look at another two short parables that describe what the Kingdom of Heaven is like…firstly, the 'hidden treasure' and secondly, the 'pearl'. These focus on the **great value** of the Kingdom.

The Hidden Treasure

"The kingdom of heaven is like treasure hidden in a field. When a man found it, he hid it again, and then in his joy went and sold all he had and bought that field" (Matt. 13:44).

This parable of the 'hidden treasure' is only found in Matthew, who was writing to Jewish Christians as a Rabbinic parallel. Rabbis taught something similar by saying that a man inherits a large estate and sells it for a small amount for a quick sale. The person who bought it then finds the treasure and the original owner is angry with himself for selling it. They used this to illustrate how Pharaoh would have thought after letting the nation of Israel go. Though similar in some ways, Jesus has a very different meaning. The Rabbinic parable taught about losing out on treasure, whereas the Gospel account uses this similar parable to switch things around, for the Jewish readers to understand the great value of finding the Kingdom. In fact, so great is its value, that one should give up everything they had just to enter it.

Somebody else had already done the hard work of hiding the treasure in the first place. Likewise, Jesus did the hard work of ushering in his Kingdom and laying down his life, so that we might live in it and gain fullness of life. Back in Jesus' day, they did not have banks or secure safes to store things, like we understand banks and large 'unbreakable' vaults today. People would bury their most treasured things in the ground for safekeeping. The man is simply digging or ploughing in someone else's field when he discovers buried treasure. He stumbled upon it by chance. He was not even looking for it. When he finds it, he desires above everything else to become the legitimate owner of the field because of his discovery. **Jesus is the greatest treasure** that we too somehow stumbled across, and **he is the ruler** (the owner) **of his Kingdom** (the field).

If our children were out playing and digging up the garden and uncovered some great treasure chest, we would be totally motivated, upbeat and would sprint down the garden towards it with great joy. When you glimpse Jesus, you discover the most precious thing on earth and should run to him with great joy. When you encounter this incredible King personally everything changes: your perspective on faith, on hope, on love and on life itself. Encountering King Jesus is not just a nice thing to have, or an add-on to your collection of life's experiences, rather it's a complete overhaul of who you are and why you exist! There is also the realisation that you can personally know, and live a life walking with, the King of kings. We can't do this thing called Christian faith without the King – that would just be religion. It is only when we meet the King and get to know him, through the indwelling Holy Spirit, that we can live out the things he asks us to do through relationship and in loving obedience.

Next, the man decides to hide the treasure again. Then he runs off and purchases the land for its regular price. Please note that the parable is not about the moral ethics of this man being a bit sneaky, knowing he would gain much more than he actually paid. What the parable is about is to explain **the magnitude of the value of this Kingdom**. The man was so desperate to secure the land and its treasure, that he would sell everything he had so that he could gain it...the Kingdom! He was willing to give up everything to be a part of it.

In Conclusion

How about you? Do you value the Kingdom of Heaven above everything else? I wonder how desperate we are as disciples of Jesus to be in, and to fully live for his Kingdom? What do you need to give up, or let go of, or put down, so that you can walk closer with the King? What things do you value more than him...your family, your home, your business? Perhaps God is prompting you right now, and asking you to sacrifice something today, so that you can truly... *"seek first his Kingdom"* (Matt. 6:33). My advice: listen, and then joyfully obey.

CHAPTER FIVE

A Pearl

The parable about a 'pearl' also focuses on the **great value** of the Kingdom, so are we getting the message?

The Pearl

"Again, the kingdom of heaven is like a merchant looking for fine pearls. When he found one of great value, he went away and sold everything he had and bought it" (Matt. 13:45-46).

This parable of the 'pearl' is also only found in Matthew. This time a merchant who has been searching and searching finally finds what he has been looking for: a fine pearl of great value that is a supreme treasure. He has stopped at nothing and left no stone unturned to secure it.

In the ancient world, pearls were extremely desirable for their beauty, their feel, their looks and their monetary value. A pearl was a beautiful thing to behold and the loveliest thing to own. People would search the world over to find the best ones that they possibly could. Perhaps today, your pearl would be a Ferrari or a large diamond ring?

There is a cool, hip new area in downtown San Antonio, called 'The Pearl'. It's the newest place to be seen and where you go to find some great places to eat and drink and to just hang out. It hosts the best hotel in the city and oozes with trendy coffee shops and expensive apartments. I guess that anything we know of as a pearl, or even 'The Pearl', will be of huge value.

The Kingdom of Heaven is simply and without doubt, the loveliest thing you can have in this world. It might have some **laws** (of love) to govern it and a (loving) **King** to obey, but this is a pleasure to do even if it requires sacrifice, discipline and self-denial. This is what we do when we love someone. You can have all of the loveliest things in this world, materialistically, in relationships, in work, in the arts, in sports, in travel, in experiences…but you can still miss the greatest wonder of this world.

The point is, once again, the great value of the King and his Kingdom. In the parable of the 'hidden treasure', no searching seems to have been made, the man just stumbles upon treasure. In this second and similar parable, we see a merchant who had been desperately searching for it.

Have you ever lost a phone or a wallet, a handbag, a credit card, keys or a passport? Panic sets in and we begin to search high and low and we become desperate to find these things, because they are of value to us. The Greek word used here is *zetounti* which means to search like having just lost your child. That's the type of searching that the merchant was doing – desperate searching!

What is your experience? Did you simply stumble upon Jesus and gain entry to his Kingdom or did you have to search and search to find him? For me, I found him easily enough and gained access, but I still had to search and search over many years to learn how to accurately hear his voice and to experience the heavenly realm. The searching never stops, and the seeking should remain desperate.

In Conclusion

The common thing we see between the man (hidden treasure) and the merchant (pearl) is that they sold everything. It meant that much to them; it was so precious. How can we possibly just be Sunday Christians by way of comparison? I wonder if some in the Church have lost the true value of Jesus today. The distractions of what we already have, alongside the things that we are seeking to get, certainly don't help us. At times we can go from Monday to Saturday, working and so consumed with all kinds of 'stuff', that Jesus is hardly able to get a look in! Surely that's not how it's meant to be. It's time to put aside the distractions and to seek God again with all your heart. Please do pay attention to what the Holy Spirit is prompting you about right now, in this regard.

In the bigger picture of Matthew's Gospel, there has been a growing opposition against the good news of the Kingdom, from chapter eleven onwards. Here in chapter thirteen, Jesus begins to disclose the Kingdom of Heaven in parables. The disciples had gained some insight to the spiritual nature of the Kingdom and so these parables bring them divine truth, as well as a much greater understanding of what this Kingdom is really like, by unveiling its mysteries and its secrets (Matt. 13:11).
The parables of the hidden treasure and pearl speak of the sacrificial pursuit of a single goal – Jesus!

Today, will you sell everything you have, as it were, just to get a glimpse of the King? Jesus is worth it. Living in the obedience of his present Kingdom is worth it.

CHAPTER SIX

A Net

The Kingdom of Heaven is not a pure community of believers alone. We know that we are in this world of other Kingdoms around us, but that we are not of them. This will mean that we will have to roll up our sleeves and get messy, as we engage with the lost, but as we do so, we must maintain the conduct and holy behaviour that the Kingdom exudes.

The Net

"Once again, the kingdom of heaven is like a net that was let down into the lake and caught all kinds of fish. [48] When it was full, the fishermen pulled it up on the shore. Then they sat down and collected the good fish in baskets, but threw the bad away. [49] This is how it will be at the end of the age. The angels will come and separate the wicked from the righteous [50] and throw them into the blazing furnace, where there will be weeping and gnashing of teeth" (Matt. 13:47-50).

This parable is only found in Matthew. The key point is that **when the King returns not all will be found worthy**.

This net would have been a large drag-net with weights on the bottom and floats on the top to catch many fish. It was let down into a lake (or sea) by fisherman that catch all, or every kind, of fish. This reminds me of the… *"every tribe and tongue"* found in the Book of Revelation (Rev. 5:9).

I went fishing once with a friend, having only been a couple of times in my life. Guess what? Once again, I'm far from being an expert. My friend perhaps isn't an expert fisherman either, but he certainly knew a lot more than I did. He had so much more experience than me, that I was willing to listen and learn from him. As a disciple of Jesus do you remain humble and teachable? There is always someone who can teach us some new things if we stay willing to learn.

When the net is full, the fishermen pull it up onto the shore or beach, which is not an easy task and requires a boat, along with a lot of muscle power. Next, they sort the fish, putting the good ones in baskets and the bad ones they simply throw away.

The picture is one we can imagine even if we have never been fishing. It is used to help us understand what the angels will do with the people of this world. It also reminds me of the sheep and goats (Matt. 25:31-33) or the end-time harvest (Rev. 7:9), which our current text goes on to confirm. This is most certainly what will happen.

Notice that the good fish and the bad fish are caught in the same net, which represents the Kingdom. We saw this earlier in the parable of the wheat and weeds, where God allows good and bad to exist side by in his Kingdom, that hovers over this entire planet. This parable of the net compliments and also confirms that the real people of the Kingdom are found along with those who don't actually belong to it.

Again, make no mistake, angels will, in the end, separate the righteous (who are not just 'good people' but those made right before God through accepting Jesus), from those who have not been made righteous in this way, regardless of the amount of good or evil that they may have done. The little old lady who has harmed no-one all her life or the crazed axe murderer! You have to be made righteous and only Jesus can do this; he puts his robes of righteousness upon us when we accept him (Matt. 5:20; Rev. 22:14).

We are destined for an eternity with Jesus in heaven, if we have believed Jesus is who he claimed to be. We believe in our heart and confess this with our mouth, that Jesus is now our Lord (Rom. 10:9). Those that don't will end up in an eternity of suffering – described here as a blazing furnace. We certainly don't want to end up there and we certainly won't if we are his disciples. Good news for us, right? So why are we not warning others about not going to this very real place called hell?

In Conclusion

Fishing can be very tough and exhausting work, but we are expected to fish anyway. We work to extend the Kingdom of Heaven around us, to those who have not yet entered. While it can be tough, what motivates us is two-fold. Firstly, we know our own destination and secondly, we want to minimise the number of those who are counted as unworthy.

In the next chapter, we shall see Jesus' conclusion to these seven parables found in chapter thirteen, and how we can be classed as 'experts' in his Kingdom.

CHAPTER SEVEN

A House Owner

If I was to offer you the ability to become an expert in something that you enjoyed, well in anything actually, I imagine most of us would jump at the opportunity. That's because we know how many years of hard work it takes to become good at something let alone become an expert. Perhaps gaining a doctorate would do just fine. Often people can be experts without such a high academic standard. Are you an expert baker, watch repairer or craftsman of some sort? When we think in terms of an expert, we trust in their knowledge and understanding and we are happy to learn from them and follow their advice. From the parables we have looked at so far, I have already confessed not to be an expert in farming, gardening, cooking nor in fishing. I'm nowhere near an 'expert' level in these things.

As we look at the seventh "Kingdom of Heaven is like…" parable from Matthew chapter thirteen – would it interest you to know that **understanding just these seven parables qualifies you as an expert in the Kingdom?** Would you like to be an 'expert' in the Kingdom and for so little effort?

Later in this Kingdom Perspective Series, when we look at the 'Laws of the Kingdom', we will see how we can become 'great' in the Kingdom. However, you can be an 'expert' without being 'great'. For example, a doctor with a lousy bedside manner. He would still be an expert but overall, not a great doctor. As we build this framework of the Kingdom of Heaven, our focus at this juncture is becoming an expert. We need to be experts in understanding what the Kingdom is like, but we do still need to be great, by practising and teaching the laws of the Kingdom (Matt. 5:19; 7:24). The good news is that we can all be 'great experts'!

The House Owner

"Have you understood all these things?" Jesus asked. *"Yes,"* they replied. *[52] He said to them, "Therefore every **teacher of the law** who has become a **disciple in the kingdom of heaven** is like the **owner of a house** who **brings out** of his **storeroom** new **treasures** as well as old"* (Matt. 13:51-52).

Have you understood? The disciples say *"yes"*. Twice earlier, though (Matt. 13:10, 36), the disciples had to ask for an explanation. Jesus wants to ensure this time that they have completely grasped the meaning.

Have you understood? Jesus says that... *"every teacher of the law who has become a disciple in the Kingdom of Heaven"*; but I prefer, perhaps a better rendering of the original language offered by Prof. W. F. Slater: *"every teacher who has been instructed in the truths of the Kingdom of Heaven"*.[11] If we do now understand the key parables Jesus is wanting us to understand, including the house owner below, then we can teach them to others. Teachers of the law are the 'experts' in

---

[11] Slater, W. F. *The Gospel of Saint Matthew* (Edinburgh: T. C. & E. C. Jack Ltd., 1901).

the law able to train others to become lawyers. Likewise, we have now been through these key parables and so are instructed in the truths of the Kingdom, becoming those experts ready to teach others what we have learnt and applied in our lives.

Jesus goes on to say… "*that you are like a **house owner** who has a **storeroom** of new and old **treasures** and that you **bring them out***". To bring them out simply means to share the great news of Jesus and his Kingdom with others. You don't leave your treasures in the storeroom. Or do you keep the 'best china' hidden away and only for special occasions? Not so, with the Kingdom of Heaven. This treasure should always be out; it should always be on display in your life, in both your actions and your speech!

The house owner is someone who has the ability to distribute what is in his estate, with and to his guests… "*Freely you have received, freely give*" (Matt. 10:8). The storeroom refers to an ample store of things to share. You have ample things to share about who God is, what he has done in your life and how he has become a part of it, and now also what his Kingdom of Heaven is really like.

Treasures can be both new and old truths, that you use to meet the needs of others. The 'old' may refer to your experiences and learning, whilst the 'new' may refer to fresh spiritual revelation and new understanding. The new could also possibly mean the NT covenant teaching that enhances the OT, because Jesus came to fulfil the law, not replace it (Matt. 5:17).

Understanding to Live these Parables

The "Kingdom of Heaven is like" parables have been effective in communicating truth to the disciples; the secrets of the Kingdom having been made known to them (Matt. 13:11). This new and revelatory knowledge and understanding made them, and potentially us today, experts in the Kingdom, qualified to then explain and share them with others. This knowledge must become a 'revelation' of heart and mind, so that we actually live out these parables. You don't have to have a PhD to be an expert in the Kingdom, but you do need to know deep within, what these 'secrets' are. Secret or mystery, does not mean that it is deeply profound and difficult, but rather something that God has kept secret or hidden, is now disclosed to us.

Wouldn't it be tragic if you had tremendous skills or were an expert in something, but you never taught anyone else what you know... *"You are the light of the world. A city built on a hill cannot be hidden. Neither do people light a lamp and put it under a bowl. Instead, they put it on its stand, and it gives light to everyone in the house. In the same way, let your light shine before others, that they may see your good deeds and glorify [praise] your Father in heaven"* (Matt. 5:14-16).

In Conclusion

Have you understood? Can **you** say yes, and what difference will that make in your life? If you understand just these seven parables about the Kingdom it should change your walk with Jesus dramatically:

You should be focused on being spiritually alert and listening to God and not be unaware of the expected opposition from the Devil (1. wheat/weeds). It's called Prayer!

You should expect powerful growth within yourself and those around you, and in society at large (2. mustard seed, 3. yeast).

You should have the revelation that what you have entered is of the greatest possible value ever, whether you stumbled upon it by chance, or have had to search and search to find it (4. hidden treasure, 5. pearl). Be willing to sacrifice anything and everything to gain not just entrance, but to also continue searching desperately to encounter Father, Son and Holy Spirit – to know your God!

You should be sharing the message of the Kingdom of Heaven everywhere you can in this world (6. net).

You should bring out all the godly treasures you have in your storeroom, to help the unworthy to enter (7. house owner).

These parables have also shown that I'm not an expert farmer, gardener, cook or fisherman in the natural. That's ok though because, if I value the King and his Kingdom of Heaven above everything else, and I can tell people about it, then God will do the rest. How about you? If you ever feel that you're not good at something, or even most things, as long as you love Jesus and tell others about him then that's absolutely fine.

CHAPTER EIGHT

A King and an Unmerciful Servant

There are five further "the Kingdom of Heaven is like" parables in Matthew, beyond the seven we have looked at in chapter thirteen. After Jesus has given the secrets of how to be an expert in the Kingdom, we need next to journey on to chapter eighteen. From the end of chapter thirteen, we see on route the continued opposition to Jesus and his spiritual and powerful Kingdom. Whenever you feel some opposition from the enemy, know that you are in good company. This increasing opposition will of course, ultimately result in Jesus crucifixion (Matt. 16:21; 17:22-23), and so we see Jesus teaching and readying his disciples for his absence (Matt. 16:24-28). Herein lie sixteen passages that intersperse **conflict and faith**. Some examples would be Jesus being rejected in his home town (Matt. 13:53-58).

Chapter 14
- John the Baptist is beheaded, but then…
- Jesus feeds the five-thousand.
- Jesus walks on water.

Chapter 15
- Disciples accused of breaking the tradition of the elders on cleanliness, but then…
- Jesus heals the demon-possessed daughter of the woman from Canaan.
- Jesus feeds the four-thousand.

Chapter 16
- A sign from heaven is demanded of Jesus, who warns against the Pharisees and Sadducees, but then…
- Peter hears from heaven and confesses Jesus as the Christ.
- Jesus predicts his death, but then…

Chapter 17
- Jesus is transfigured before three disciples, giving them a temporary glimpse of his future glory.
- Jesus heals a demon-possessed boy.
- Jesus is accused of not paying taxes, but then…
- Jesus miraculously provides the tax payment.

Just before our next 'Kingdom of Heaven is like' parable in chapter eighteen, we see at the beginning of this chapter that humility like a child is what is needed to be the greatest in the Kingdom, that we must not cause others to sin, and that God will chase after the one who gets lost (Matt. 18:1-14).

Then comes a section on church discipline (Matt. 18:15-20), and it is in that context of discipline that we see the famously and often quoted scriptures of 'binding and loosing' and *"if two of you on earth agree about anything you ask for, it will be done for you"* and *"when two or three gather in my name, there I am with them"*.

I offer a very short comment on these:
God shows mercy for the one that gets lost, and then he wants us to agree on merciful resolutions to disputes.
Loosing is saying sorry and continuing in fellowship, whereas binding is not saying sorry, continuing in sin and exclusion from fellowship.

Harmony and unity bring spiritual authority, perhaps by two people agreeing in a three-person leadership. When people gather and work things through in this manner, Jesus promises to be present in that process. Often this text is used slightly out of context, to reassure smaller Christian gatherings.

It is now that Jesus adds in this parable of the unmerciful servant, to again make sure that we have understood.

The King and the Unmerciful Servant

*"Then Peter came to Jesus and asked, "Lord, how many times shall I forgive my brother or sister who sins against me? Up to seven times?" [22] Jesus answered, "I tell you, not seven times, but seventy-seven times. [23] "Therefore, **the kingdom of heaven is like** a king who wanted to settle accounts with his servants. [24] As he began the settlement, a man who owed him ten thousand bags of gold [talents] was brought to him. [25] Since he was not able to pay, the master ordered that he and his wife and his children and all that he had be sold to repay the debt. [26] "At this the servant fell on his knees before him. 'Be patient with me,' he begged, 'and I will pay back everything.' [27] The servant's master took pity on him, cancelled the debt and let him go. [28] "But when that servant went out, he found one of his fellow servants who owed him a hundred denarii [silver coins]. He grabbed him and began to choke him. 'Pay back what you owe me!' he demanded. [29] "His fellow servant fell to his knees and begged him, 'Be patient with me, and I will pay it back.' [30] "But he refused. Instead, he went off and had the man thrown into prison until he could pay the debt. [31] When the other servants saw what had happened, they were greatly distressed [outraged] and went and told their master everything that had happened. [32] "Then the master called*

the servant in. 'You wicked servant,' he said, 'I cancelled all that debt of yours because you begged me to. [33] Shouldn't you have had mercy on your fellow servant just as I had on you?' [34] In anger his master handed him over to the jailers to be tortured, until he should pay back all he owed. [35] "This is how my heavenly Father will treat each of you unless you forgive your brother or sister from your heart"" (Matt. 18:21-35).

Where there is less focus on 'discipleship growth', there may well be more discipline required. Discipline may need to be firm at times, but it also needs to done with mercy! Being disciplined should not be an issue for disciples as these two words come from the same root meaning. We also know that God, as a wonderful and loving Father, disciplines us for our own good (Heb. 12:10).

Maturity in your faith is displayed when you accept discipline with a positive attitude, wanting to grow and learn, rather than taking offence and 'throwing your toys out of the pram'. It sounds easy enough doesn't it, but often the ability to do so is all that separates leaders from followers. This is why I always look at people's heart responses to things, because that tells me a lot of what I need to know as a Pastor.

Before we delve back into our main parable please pause and think for a moment…**what is the worst thing that has been done against you?** Have you remembered that situation? I imagine that you may not like that memory, and that it was a completely unfair thing. **Should you forgive?** We will come back to this shortly.

Immediately after Jesus has said these things, about humility, not causing others to stumble, looking out for the one going astray and now merciful discipline, Peter comes to ask him how many times he should forgive someone who sins against him, and he boldly suggests seven times! **This is a pivotal Kingdom question**.

Peter had already heard Jesus teach on forgiveness in the Sermon on the Mount and knows that he has to forgive. His question, with a suggested answer of seven, is more about longsuffering. How many times should we forgive a repeat offender, or when we have been broken by the actions that others took against us? The question Peter raises does relate to the discipline process, when one person attempts to forgive and to reconcile with another (Matt. 18:21). Jesus ups the ante, with a multiplication of Peter's perhaps healthy suggestion of seven times, which is the biblical number for perfection after all. The seventy-seven times (some Bible translations use seventy times seven) is the opposite of the seventy-seven that Lamech boasted about, the number of times he would avenge himself upon anyone who injures him (Gen. 4:15, 23-24). It's not an exact number of times, but what Jesus is saying, is to 'think bigger'. You are empowered to forgive and it is a choice, so **see forgiveness as something that is unending until you are free**, free that is, from any negative emotional response from the person, situation or pain that was caused (Matt. 18:22).

In this parable, the King wishes to settle accounts with his servants. Settling accounts could mean paying some money to them for wages, but in this story, it is to collect money that he was owed. The servant somehow owes the King ten-thousand talents, which was an astonishing amount of debt. One simply could not pay this off in a lifetime of working every single day. We are not told how this servant came to owe such a huge and crippling debt, but we can still certainly recognise today the crippling feeling that debt can have over us. It sounds like bankruptcy is imminent but the worst possible kind, as every single possession is to be sold, including selling the servants wife and children into slavery. Today our homes might still get repossessed and we can lose material things, but imagine having to sell your loved ones (Matt. 18:23-25).

The man begs for patience, for more time, so that he can at least try to pay back this impossible debt. Will the King show him mercy? Yes, he does. The servant's master (who is the King) takes pity on him and instead of allowing more time for the servant to pay, the King shows astonishing mercy and cancels the debt in full and lets him and his family go free – wow! Normally in this situation, the whole family would all have become slaves. The servant literally now has ten-thousand reasons to bless the Lord, just like in that famous worship song we perhaps have heard and sung.

You know, God has forgiven us so very much and he has paid the highest possible price himself, by sacrificing his one and only Son. He did this so that we could not only be forgiven our sin, but made righteous and holy before the Father, because of the cross. He did it so that we could live a life of freedom, fullness and abundance, an adventure with Father, Son and Spirit in extending his Kingdom (Matt. 18:26-27).

The unmerciful servant then goes straight out from the King's presence and finds another servant who owes him a small debt (about three months' wages). He is violent towards him and demands everything owed to him. With all this in mind – how will you (and I) now treat your brother or sister who offends you, whether they meant to hurt you or not? Do you hold onto the debt and grief caused against you? This other servant also begs for patience, just as the unmerciful servant did himself only moments earlier (Matt. 18:28-29).

How sad that the unmerciful servant not only refuses to show mercy towards someone else, but he also throws the 'rule book' at him. He has him thrown into jail until the debt can be repaid. He certainly did not follow the 'Golden Rule' (Matt. 7:12) of doing to others as you would have them to do you. Some other servants are witnesses to all this that took place and they cannot believe the hypocrisy. They are so distressed that they go to the master (the King) and tell him what has happened. If you happen to think that other people around you cannot see your double-mindedness, you would be wrong. Not only in the Church, but even more so, those who are in the world (Matt. 18:30-31).

Now the King is a 'little bit upset' and calls the unmerciful servant back in. He tells him, in no uncertain terms, that he is rather wicked. The Greek word used is *poneros* meaning evil, bad, wicked, and malicious. The King states that he cancelled all of the unmerciful servant's debt, because he begged him to. The King tells him he should have shown mercy just like he the servant had been shown great mercy. An angry King now reverses his decision, reinstates the debt and then turns the unmerciful servant over to the jailors. But now things are even worse, as the unmerciful servant will be imprisoned and tortured, the Greek word used for tortured is *basanistes*, meaning a tormentor or one who tortured…for the rest of his life! This does sound like, and is, a living hell. His unmerciful and unforgiving way has led to him legally being tortured and tormented. In the same way, our unmerciful and unforgiving behaviour allows the enemy a legal foothold in our lives to torment us. This can quickly become a stronghold which is something that we may find almost impossible to break free from (Matt. 18:32-34).

The unmerciful servant had gained his initial forgiveness through a hoax or false pretence. We must not pretend when it comes to forgiveness. This parable shows us how God will allow us to be treated unless we forgive others from the heart. He will allow us to be tormented by the enemy.

In Conclusion

There is a clear link between this parable and the Lord's prayer in Matthew 6:14. **We must at least, always remain willing to forgive. It must be genuine and from the heart. This kind of forgiveness must rule amongst the disciples of Jesus**. Mercy should be shown in relationships amongst us as a church, and also into the wider community around us. We should not be hardnosed, unloving and dictatorial in dealing with people. Remember that mercy triumphs over judgment (James 2:13).

The motivating factor in showing mercy and forgiveness is the incredible love that our heavenly Father displays towards us.

God has had to forgive, and continues to forgive, far more than we will ever have to (Matt. 18:35).

It can be difficult to reconcile the discipline process and unlimited forgiveness. As disciples, we should know that someone in authority may need to lovingly bring discipline for our benefit. Yet at the same time, we should be forgiving people endlessly, so that we can be free to live the lives of abundance that Jesus offers us.

In the Kingdom of Heaven, we must not easily take offence and we must not hold on to un-forgiveness, which leads to bitterness. So…who was it that hurt you the most? Who do you need to forgive? Who do you need to show mercy to, even if they don't deserve it?

I hope that you are able to see how much you have been forgiven and the essential need for you to also forgive. It's your freedom that is at stake.

CHAPTER NINE

Workers in the Vineyard

In chapter nineteen of Matthew, we find the next "the Kingdom of Heaven is like" parable. Jesus travels on to the region of Judea to minister there and he speaks in front of large crowds: 1) about divorce where the Pharisees attempt to trick him and Jesus says that some will even renounce marriage for the Kingdom of Heaven, 2) about accepting little children that are pure and humble, and that the Kingdom of Heaven belongs to such as these, and 3) about it being hard for the rich to enter the Kingdom (Matt. 19:1-22).

Jesus then huddles the disciples in together to speak in more detail with them… *"Then Jesus said to his disciples, "I tell you the truth, it is hard for someone who is rich to enter the kingdom of heaven. ²⁴ Again I tell you, it is easier for a camel to go through the eye of a needle than for someone who is rich to enter the kingdom of God." ²⁵ When the disciples heard this, they were greatly astonished and asked, "Who then can be saved?" ²⁶ Jesus looked at them and said, "With man this is impossible, but with God all things are possible." ²⁷ Peter answered him, "We have left everything to follow you!* **What then will there be for us?"** *²⁸ Jesus said to them, "I tell you the truth, at the renewal of all things, when the Son of Man sits on his glorious throne,* **you who have followed me will also sit on twelve thrones, judging the twelve tribes of Israel.** *²⁹ And everyone who has left houses or brothers or sisters or father or mother or children or fields for my* *sake **will receive a hundred times as much and will inherit eternal life**. [30] But many who are first will be last, and many who are last will be first"""* (Matt. 19:23-30).

The rich people in our world do seem to have it all don't they – money and the 'good life'. Matthew records Jesus speaking to a rich young man who unfortunately places his money above the Kingdom of Heaven (Matt. 19:16-22). Jesus then makes some remarkable statements in our main text above – using twelve thrones and judging the twelve tribes of Israel – for the disciples to grasp what they will receive. The words of Jesus would have simply astonished them! Anyone else will receive a hundred times as much and inherit eternal life. Basically, he is saying that when you are in the Kingdom of Heaven you will get far more than you could ever have imagined. Your reward will far outweigh any present suffering or sacrifice.

Compared to the rich young man, the disciples have given up everything to follow Jesus and so in worldly terms, they are 'last', but they will end up 'first'. There will be a reversal of things. Jesus will take care of your future.

Have you ever felt that you have been overlooked for a promotion? Perhaps you felt like you were not being rewarded fully for the work and effort you had been giving. I have worked for many years in the IT industry for some very large multinational companies. At one, I ended up feeling aggrieved because I was paid less than some of my colleagues; at another, I gained unexpected promotion; in another, I again felt aggrieved as the responsibility and expected effort far outweighed the reward. I guess many of you will resonate with these types of situations, but my point is: when things went the way I wanted them to, I was happy, but when they didn't my heart attitude was not, let's say, at its best! In the Kingdom of Heaven however, it is essential that disciples of Jesus **maintain the right heart of devotion, throughout their sacrificial service.**

Jesus now brings the parable of the 'workers in the vineyard', to help practically illustrate this right heart of devotion. In doing so Jesus continues to answer Peter's question…**what will there be for us?** What will there be for you and I in the Kingdom of Heaven? The division of chapters nineteen and twenty at this point is unhelpful, as it causes us to think of these separately, when they should remain joined together.

The Workers in the Vineyard

*"For **the kingdom of heaven is like a landowner** who went out early in the morning to hire workers for his vineyard. ² He agreed to pay them a denarius for the day and sent them into his vineyard. ³ "About nine in the morning he went out and saw others standing in the marketplace doing nothing. ⁴ He told them, 'You also go and work in my vineyard, and I will pay you whatever is right.' ⁵ So they went. "He went out again about noon and about three in the afternoon and did the same thing. ⁶ About five in the afternoon he went out and found still others standing around. He asked them, 'Why have you been standing here all day long doing nothing?' ⁷ "'Because no one has hired us,' they answered. "He said to them, 'You also go and work in my vineyard.' ⁸ "When evening came, the owner of the vineyard said to his foreman, 'Call the workers and pay them their wages, beginning with the last ones hired and going on to*

the first.' ⁹ "The workers who were hired about five in the afternoon came and each received a denarius. ¹⁰ So when those came who were hired first, they expected to receive more. But each one of them also received a denarius. ¹¹ When they received it, they began to grumble against the landowner. ¹² 'These who were hired last worked only one hour,' they said, 'and you have made them equal to us who have borne the burden of the work and the heat of the day.' ¹³ "But he answered one of them, 'I am not being unfair to you, friend. Didn't you agree to work for a denarius? ¹⁴ Take your pay and go. I want to give the one who was hired last the same as I gave you. ¹⁵ Don't I have the right to do what I want with my own money? Or are you envious because I am generous?' ¹⁶ "So the last will be first, and the first will be last"" (Matt. 20:1-16).

A landowner is someone with wealth, power, control and dominion over his land and all that happens within it. Sounds a bit like a King and his Kingdom. This landowner went out early to hire some workers, probably so they could start work by 6am; and he agrees a normal day's pay with them: a denarius. By 9am he sees people not yet hired so he hires them as well, saying he will pay them **whatever is right**, and he had probably already decided in his heart to be generous and to pay them the same, even though they had missed the first part of the day.

He does the exact same thing at 12pm and 3pm as well. I do wonder if he was getting more excited each time he went, knowing that he planned a larger and larger blessing each time. Perhaps he knew that it is more blessed to give than to receive (Acts 20:35). He was about to show huge generosity to a whole bunch of people, a bit like a parent ready and waiting to give Christmas presents to their child, knowing what is inside.

This also reminds me of the show 'Undercover Boss'. In each episode, a corporate CEO leaves his usual high position for a week, and goes back to working 'on the shop floor', but in disguise. This is so that he or she will not be recognised by any of the employees, often using an excuse about the film crew following and making a documentary on entry-level jobs. At the end of the week, the employees who worked closely with the disguised CEO, are called into Head Office without reason. They turn up nervous and wondering if they will be keeping their jobs. Next, the now undisguised CEO walks in and reveals to these unsuspecting employees who he or she really is. They now put 'two and two together' and recognise that this CEO is the same person that they had just been helping on the shop floor. The CEO, now knows first-hand some of the work and personal struggles that his employees face. Knowing some of their issues and difficulties at work and home, having rubbed shoulders with them over the previous week, the CEO then promises to fix processes in the business, but also unleashes some great generosity with bonuses, sponsorships, extra holidays and promotions. Everyone usually ends up in tears (including me) because of the love and kindness being displayed, with one person really helping to meet the needs of another.

The landowner goes back at 5pm near the end of the day and still finds people who had not been hired. Why do you think they had not been hired? Were they lazy or something? Would these people have been the worst possible employees? Most likely, they would have been the outcasts and the marginalised of their society. This landowner, however, makes absolutely no distinction between them and the others that he has already hired. He does not label them and he does not reject them. He looks past any prejudice and hires them as well. He makes no judgement towards them and simply sends them into his vineyard, just as he has been doing all day long.

Interestingly, it was only the first people hired that the landowner had agreed how much he would pay: a day's wage of a denarius. All the rest would have assumed that they would receive something, but only a part of a day's wage. The 5pm hires would probably expect that they would get only an hour's pay. Evening comes and the landowner gets his foreman to call in the workers from the vineyard at the end of the day, to pay them their wages, but starting with the last. The 5pm hires, the 'last', come in 'first', and incredibly they get a full day's wage for an hour's work – astonishing! Who wouldn't like that sort of deal? Perhaps we need to dig a bit deeper, so that we can see the real significance, by putting ourselves into the shoes of the 5pm hires. They will have sat there in that marketplace all day. Outside of the vineyard, they would have been hot, miserable, stressed about how to pay their bills and feed their families. All hope is lost for them, and perhaps reality dawns that there will again be no food on the table that night. They feel useless and worthless. Then, 'completely out of the blue', they are amazed to have someone come and hire them, so at least they will get something. They do their best for the last hour of the working day. Because of their usual rejection as outcasts, they are already delighted to now be able to at least put some food on the table. But when the foreman calls them in, they end up even more astonished to receive a full day's wage for an hour of their labour. What rejoicing! Did you notice that it was the foreman who gave them their wages? The landowner did not seek any praise or glory for himself.

Many people today spend the majority of their lives outside of the Kingdom of Heaven. Living in fear and often without hope, joy or peace. Locked into a secular world without real meaning. They, like the 5pm hires, will rejoice extravagantly because they have finally come into the Kingdom of Heaven. At last, they are accepted just as much as those who have spent their entire lives in this Kingdom. They are given equal pay and equal benefits. Just like the 5pm hires in this parable.

Those who had been in the vineyard (or Kingdom) longer, those who arrived first, the 6am, 9am, 12pm and 3pm hires, suddenly expect more pay and benefits than they had already agreed upon or had now come to expect, all because they see the incredible generosity of the landowner. However, they have lost sight of something here. Instead of an appreciation for just being part of the vineyard (or Kingdom) and working to serve the landowner (or King), they have become jealous of those who have now been given the same entitlement that they have. They begin to grumble against the landowner, that they have been made equal with those who have done less. Well, guess what folks, if you are in the Kingdom of Heaven then you are equal before God with everyone else. There are no superstars in the Kingdom, only a super King.

The world around us craves for equality. In pay, across gender and race, and with rights and privileges. Honestly, I don't think it will ever truly happen. Why? Not because I don't want it to, but because of greed and power, we will never have an equal world. However, in the Kingdom of Heaven, we see that all are equal. Whether it is those who have spent their whole lives following Jesus or those who are the latest recruits; all are equal.

The landowner says he is not being unfair, but rather he is showing the same love and generosity to all. He is the one with the wealth and he gets to decide how he will spend it. Jesus is the King and chooses to show the same love and generosity to all. It is his Kingdom and he gets to choose how it operates. He remains good and he treats people fairly and very generously. So, the *"last will be first"* and the *"first will be last"*. Keeping our text that straddles these two chapters adjoined, it is easier to remember that the rich young man who is 'first' ends up 'last', and that the disciples who are 'last' end up 'first'. Now that the disciples realise that they are first, the learning point for them is that **they must maintain the right heart of devotion in their service for Jesus.**

In Conclusion

The workers were hired 'first to last' but paid 'last to first', and this is a warning never to presume how God's grace will be shown to others. The disciples must not seek reward, but rather their King, and the same applies to us today as well.

What will there be for us? The King does promise us reward. We already have the hope that we are in the Kingdom of Heaven, and for an incredible future and journey ahead. We know that we will receive far more than we can imagine, including eternal life, and blessings beyond measure and a life of walking in close devotion and relationship with our God. **There is no higher reward**. However, can you say that you **always** maintain the right heart of devotion through your sacrificial service? I think we do all struggle at times, but this parable is here to remind us how very blessed we really are, as the basis upon which we serve Jesus, with the very best heart attitude that we can.

Maintaining the right heart of devotion is how the Kingdom works efficiently and effectively. You have the ability and choice to serve with willing joy, or through gritted teeth and with mutterings under your breath! Perhaps you have not been appreciated, thanked or encouraged as you served, and even made to feel like the 5pm hire. While that remains regrettable and unfortunate, it is only you, however, who can maintain your heart attitude. This parable will help remind you of your astonishing reward. Never let this fact slip. Use it to maintain your true devotion and continued service for Jesus, even when pastors and leaders unintentionally make these kinds of mistakes. The Kingdom of Heaven remains a Kingdom of devotion to Jesus, and one of right attitudes when serving him.

CHAPTER TEN

A Wedding Feast

Now we move on to the next "the Kingdom of Heaven is like" parable in Matthew – the parable of the wedding feast. A few notable things happen before we get there…

Next in Matthew chapter twenty, Jesus begins the journey to Jerusalem (Matt. 20:17) and he tells the disciples, for the third time, that he will be crucified, die and three days later be raised to life!

If we consider that Jesus has just told the parable of the 'workers in the vineyard', we know he is wanting the disciples to maintain the right heart attitude. If we also consider, that Jesus has now said for the third time he is about to sacrifice his life, it is quite incredible that the next thing to happen is a request from a mother and two of her sons, for these two sons to be able to sit on the right and left of Jesus in the Kingdom (Matt. 20:21). It looks a bit like the lead up to an election, where everyone is politically jostling and fighting for power and for the best position they can get. Paraphrasing the response, Jesus says "shhh you muppets, that is Papa's job to decide!" The other disciples are just a 'little miffed', and so Jesus calms the situation saying that to be great, you must be a servant.

Next, Jesus and his disciples head out from Jericho, which is only about fifteen miles from Jerusalem (Matt. 20:29). On route, Jesus demonstrates compassion by hearing the cry of two blind men, who he then heals. Are you crying out to God for his attention like these two blind men? I wonder if these things are linked, i.e. the right heart attitude that cries out to God (even if in desperation), is the heart that will capture God's attention, and bring him into your situation.

"As they approached Jerusalem, they came to Bethphage on the Mount of Olives" (Matt. 21:1). Jesus then enters Jerusalem as a King riding on a donkey and... "the whole city was stirred" (Matt. 21:10). It takes a major event to stir a city so this was a very significant happening. Today, it would be a major city sporting event like a marathon, a Cup Final or the latest and greatest pop band playing a concert. The first thing Jesus does after his arrival is to cleanse the temple of those corruptly trading there (Matt. 21:12-13). The following day as he is teaching the Jewish people and his disciples, again in the temple (Matt. 21:23), he uses the parable of the 'two sons' and the 'tenants' to denounce the Chief Priests and Pharisees. Jesus does this because they question his authority and because they produce no fruit. The Kingdom will be given to a people who will produce its fruit (Matt. 21:43). Fruits plural are to be produced in us: love, joy, peace, patience, kindness, goodness, faithfulness, gentleness and self-control (Gal. 5:22). We should grow in all of these areas, not just in one or two of them, or only in the ones we prefer.

Quite a lot has now transpired since the parable of the workers in the vineyard, but we finally get to...

The Parable of the Wedding Feast

"Jesus spoke to them again in parables, saying: [2] *"**The kingdom of heaven is like a king** who prepared a wedding banquet for his son.* [3] *He sent his **servants** to those who had been **invited** to the **banquet** to tell them to come, but they refused to come.* [4] *"Then he sent some more servants and said, 'Tell those who have been invited that I have prepared my dinner: My oxen and fattened cattle have been butchered, and everything is ready. Come to the wedding banquet.'* [5] *"But they paid no attention and went off— one to his field, another to his business.* [6] *The rest seized his servants, mistreated them and killed them.* [7] *The king was enraged. He sent his army and destroyed those murderers and burned their city.* [8] *"Then he said to his servants, 'The wedding banquet is ready, but those I invited did not deserve to come.* [9] *So go to the street corners and invite to the banquet anyone you find.'* [10] *So the servants went out into the streets and gathered all the people they could find, the bad as well as the good, and the wedding hall was filled with guests.* [11] *"But when the king came in to see the guests, he noticed a man there who was not wearing wedding clothes.* [12] *He asked, 'How did you get in here without wedding clothes, friend?' The man was speechless.* [13] *"Then the king told the attendants, 'Tie him hand and foot, and throw him outside, into the darkness, where there will be weeping and gnashing of teeth.'* [14] *"For many are invited, but few are chosen""* (Matt. 22:1-14).

Have you ever had to prepare a party for someone? You will know very well the stress and work involved. But this goes up a whole other level if you have ever had to prepare a wedding. So much goes into the special day from things like the chapel, the service, dress wear, room layout and decorations, worship, communion, invitations, flowers, certificates, readings, food, presentations, speeches, games, presents and cake to name a few! I have personally had this 'joy' recently, but let's get on with the parable itself.

Jesus is still teaching the Jewish people in the temple with his disciples, but with the Pharisees and Chief Priests also present, so he continues to use parables. Weddings are wonderful occasions, so why is it that Jesus now begins to talk about a wedding banquet? The end of his life is fast approaching and it's getting closer to his crucifixion. What will his future be and what will that therefore mean, for our future? Jesus uses familiar language to help explain the Kingdom. He has used seven parables in chapter thirteen, the unmerciful servant in chapter eighteen, the workers in the vineyard in chapter twenty and so now this is the tenth such description. In this parable, a King wishes to prepare a wedding banquet for his son. We have no clue as to who the bride might be, but we will come back to that later.

The King sends out his servants to gather in all those who had been invited. That is amazing for two reasons: 1) the King should not have to send his servants for them at all, as people should be overjoyed to be able to attend, and 2) the fact that even with hand delivered invites the people are still unwilling to go.

If you had been invited to a banquet by Queen Elizabeth II, would any of you refuse to go? No, we would drop just about anything to go to Buckingham Palace for dinner with the

Queen, but imagine if the invite was for the recent wedding banquet for Prince Harry! We would go excitedly and without delay, we would respond to the call of the Queen. We have all received a call from Jesus the King. The question is though, how are we responding?

The King tries again and more servants are sent out to entice the invited guests. He even lets them know that they will have the best food in the land. This really will be a banquet of the finest order...not just our favourite local carvery! He lets them know that all the preparations have been made, the hard work and stress is complete, and all you have to do is just turn up. Unbelievably they are still not interested. One goes casually to his field and one to his business venture. Perhaps they don't realise it, but they are in fact being **disloyal** to their King (Matt. 22:1-5).

We see not just those that are being disloyal to the King, but also those who mistreat and kill the King's servants. Who would do such a thing? This is treachery! If our own Queen's aides personally brought you such an invitation and then later came back a second time to remind you, you would probably invite them in for a cuppa. You wouldn't mistreat them, let alone kill them. When we take out the message of the Kingdom, we too can feel like we are being mistreated by those to whom we go, because of their **indifference to Jesus**. The truth is, we need to obey the call to go. As we do, we work with the Holy Spirit allowing him to deal with any personal issues of rejection. Honestly, I don't think we receive **violent hostility** in the western world when we go. So we should certainly still go, not in fear, but much rather in faith. The King is a tad annoyed and sends his army to destroy the murderers and burns down their city. Don't mess with the King. Around four decades later, in AD70, Jerusalem is destroyed and the temple is burnt down, and don't forget that there is still a judgement day to come for all of mankind (Matt. 22:6-7).

The King sends his servants out a third time. Oh, how the religious do not deserve to come into the Kingdom, particularly as they prevent others from entering, by their laws and judgements. Now the servants invite everyone else. Not the religious and perhaps those in the most privileged positions, but those who may even have seemed unworthy of the banquet. Notice though who does the inviting? It's the servants! Who are the servants in the Kingdom today? Disciples – that's you and me. We are all supposed to be going out and inviting the lost to come to the banquet. That means to meet Jesus and not necessarily coming to a church building – although it might. But you can go, you can lead someone to Christ and you can then also bring them to the family of saints when they gather. They were obedient and went out and invited the good and the bad until the banquet, gathering, church was full. Does it say anywhere that it is the job of the pastor to do the inviting? No. Or is it the evangelist's job to do the inviting? No. It is everyone's job as a disciple to invite people until your gathering place is full and overflowing. Both the good and the bad here, shows that people do not have to be spotless or perfect or even clean to be invited. That is just as well, otherwise we would never have been invited either (Matt. 22:8-10).

The King at the banquet then spots a man who was not wearing wedding clothes and wonders how he got in. The King finds this quite insulting. When challenged by the King, this person is stunned into silence because he cannot explain his inappropriate attire. He is punished and the servants throw him outside. **The Kingdom of Heaven is open to all – but not all belong in the Kingdom**. I think God knows who is and who isn't in the Kingdom and people cannot fake it with him. Just because we go to church on Sunday, does not mean we have made it into the Kingdom. We must be born again (or born of the Spirit of God) and obey the call to grow and to go. Many are invited, the whole world in fact, but few are chosen. As you read these words have you made your choice? If you have become part of the chosen, you do still need to respond in loving obedience (Matt. 22:11-14).

In Conclusion

The invitation to the wedding banquet is to the world, both good and bad. We as disciples, are the ones to do the inviting and know that not all will respond well. Some may be disloyal, some indifferent, some even violently disposed towards us. People don't need to be perfect or of a certain standing to be invited. Not all who respond to the invitation will make it into the Kingdom of Heaven, but we should invite them anyway.

The Kingdom of Heaven is like a King who makes a way for all to attend the wedding of his son and his bride. The bride refers to the Bride of Christ (the Church) and the call is to those who choose to follow Jesus. **The call of our King Jesus requires a response**.

Prominent in this parable, is the failure of the religious to respond to God's call. How will you respond to God's call? Will you attend the wedding banquet now? In other words, will you respond now to the Kingdom which you have joined? We must not sit back and just wait for the banquet when we get to heaven. **We are called now, to affect the Kingdom of Heaven on earth**. A Kingdom of Spirit-filled power and not just words! Whatever it is that God has called you to do in his Kingdom, respond well. So how do we respond well?

According to the parable of the wedding feast:

You should say **yes wholeheartedly** to the invitation.

You should never be disloyal, indifferent or opposed to what **God is doing in you.**

You should make sure you are appropriate in **authentic relationship** to Jesus.

You should obey the call **to grow**, in the Spirit and in fruit, and **to go** and tell others.

You should walk with Jesus and **serve him now** with whatever gifts and abilities he has given you.

You should not put things off until a more convenient time!

CHAPTER ELEVEN

Ten Virgins

Jesus has told his disciples for the third time that he will be condemned to die, and from chapter twenty-one onwards, we see that Jesus has entered Jerusalem and moved into the last part of his earthly ministry. Jesus gives the parable of the wedding banquet in chapter twenty-two, that requires a response from each one called into his Kingdom of Heaven.

The religious leaders are not best pleased with Jesus and begin to plot, with an evil intent, to trap Jesus in his words (Matt. 22:15). They try using difficult questions such as whether is it right to pay taxes to Caesar (Matt. 22:17), about marriage after the resurrection (Matt. 22:28), and then about the greatest commandment (Matt. 22:36). Jesus simply outsmarts them and they are left amazed (Matt. 22:22) and astonished (Matt. 22:33) and speechless (Matt. 22:46), by his understanding and wisdom.

Speaking to the crowds in chapter twenty-three, Jesus brings seven woes against these religious leaders… *"Woe to you, teachers of the law and Pharisees, you hypocrites!"* This is all because **they do not practise what they preach** (Matt. 23:3). We in the Kingdom of Heaven are to practise its laws (Matt. 5, 6 and 7). The world is very quick to spot a hypocrite. If we talk and talk all about the laws of the Kingdom, but never practise them with our behaviour, we stand out like a sore thumb. We must practise what we preach. Jesus calls them blind guides, snakes and broods of vipers. I found out recently on a trip to Uganda that vipers are the most poisonous of snakes…it's ok though, I was in a zoo!

In chapter twenty-four, Jesus leaves the temple area and is with his disciples when he describes to them the signs of the end of the age. In this, he is telling them to be **watchful** (Matt. 24:42) and to be **ready** (Matt. 24:44). It is to drive home this point to his disciples, of being watchful and ready, that he then uses the parable of the ten virgins at the beginning of chapter twenty-five.

What kind of things have you had to get yourself ready for – perhaps events like a sports game, or acting in a play, or to give a speech, or perhaps for exams or job interviews? **To be ready for anything you have to prepare.** If you prepare well you have a better chance of success. I wanted to be ready for my wedding and this meant that I had to prepare. I took advice and counsel from other ministers and friends. Even though I have taken others through pre-marriage counselling, I still watched hours of teaching on marriage and read books myself. Alice and I even flew from the UK to Hungary to spend two days with missionary friends, who specialise in relationship ministry. It took time and effort. We had to prepare in so many ways – not just a dress and a suit and some rings. We did this because we wanted our marriage to be a success and, with God's help, we got ourselves ready.

The Parable of the Ten Virgins

"At that time the kingdom of heaven will be like ten virgins who took their lamps and went out to meet the bridegroom. ² Five of

them were foolish and five were wise. ³ The foolish ones took their lamps but did not take any oil with them. ⁴ The wise ones, however, took oil in jars along with their lamps. ⁵ The bridegroom was a long time in coming, and they all became drowsy and fell asleep. ⁶ At midnight the cry rang out: 'Here's the bridegroom! Come out to meet him!' ⁷ Then all the virgins woke up and trimmed their lamps. ⁸ The foolish ones said to the wise, 'Give us some of your oil; our lamps are going out.' ⁹ 'No,' they replied, 'there may not be enough for both us and you. Instead, go to those who sell oil and buy some for yourselves.' ¹⁰ But while they were on their way to buy the oil, the bridegroom arrived. The virgins who were ready went in with him to the wedding banquet. And the door was shut. ¹¹ Later the others also came, 'Lord, Lord,' they said, 'open the door for us!' ¹² But he replied, 'Truly I tell you, I don't know you.' ¹³ Therefore keep watch, because you do not know the day or the hour" (Matt. 25:1-13).

The first verse begins with 'at that time' or 'then', so Jesus is talking about his recent words spoken in chapter twenty-four, about the end of the age and when he will return. He likens that time to ten virgins who all had lamps and who take them as they go to meet the bridegroom – a slightly unusual sort of story. There are ten ladies here, but are they all getting married to the same bridegroom? Why were they all together, and why did they go to meet the bridegroom, instead of being escorted to the wedding by their fathers? That's what we usually do. Perhaps they are not all getting married but participating as bridesmaids for example. That would make more sense.

Some translations add in the words 'and the bride', translating it as… *"they go out to meet the bridegroom 'and the bride'".*

Although this would clear things up for us, it is not in the original Greek, and could be even more confusing if you consider that the bride in scripture usually represents the Bride of Christ, the Church. All that said, I think the ten virgins, whether they are getting married or are bridesmaids, simply represent the ones who Jesus as the bridegroom returns for. Perhaps that is why the bride herself is not mentioned and is not the usual central figure.

Jewish custom though, was a little different to the way we do things today. First, a man and woman would get **engaged** in a settlement between their fathers. Next would come the **betrothal** ceremony, when mutual promises were made before witnesses. The couple were then bound to one another even though they were not yet man and wife. It was not permitted to cancel a betrothal and doing so would be considered along the lines of divorce. Finally, after a lapse that could be as long as a year in time, there would be a **marriage**. The bridegroom would have been busy preparing, possibly building a home for himself and his new wife to live in. He would then go and fetch his bride from her father's house, to take her to their home, where the wedding feast would take place. Now the parable begins to make more sense. The ten virgins were going out to meet the bridegroom, who was coming for his betrothed, to take his bride to the wedding feast.

We see that five of them are a little foolish and five of them are wise. I'm reminded of some childhood books that I read called the 'Famous Five'; well here we have the 'Foolish Five'. The foolish five took their lamps, but they had no additional oil. They had some oil in their lamps because later, in verse eight, they say that their lamps are going out. They had some but not enough; they had not prepared properly. Now if you are thinking 'aren't they daft', let me ask you, have you ever run out of petrol? Not so daft now are they. The wise five had some extra to carry, because they took oil in jars with them as well (Matt. 25:1-4).

The bridegroom was a long time coming and all ten of them fall asleep. Christendom has waited two-thousand years for the bridegroom to return. Personally, we have waited, for all of the time that we have been Christians, for the bridegroom to return. Because he hasn't yet returned, we can easily fall asleep. In other words, we can live without any expectation of his arrival in the present moment. His return is often not at the forefront of our minds today and so we don't think, we don't prepare and we are not ready for his return. Suddenly at midnight, a shout goes up that the bridegroom is on his way. It is midnight! What on earth is he doing coming at that sort of time? Weddings are usually during the daytime, so he was certainly rather late. Today we allow the bride to turn up late don't we – ten minutes, fifteen minutes…an hour! This guy was ridiculously late for a wedding and that's an understatement. All ten wake up and trim their lamps to get them alight. I guess they needed their lamps to see at night, to actually see the bridegroom (Matt. 25:5-7).

The foolish five ask the wise five for some oil, which represents everything they needed to be ready. The wise five say no, get your own. In fact, the language used could be even more emphatic – never! There are some things we cannot borrow from others. Things like character, authenticity and integrity.

There are some things we must work out for ourselves, like our own walk with God and our own faith in him. The advice the wise five give is also rather interesting, because it was midnight! Where could the foolish five go and buy more oil, unless they had 24/7 opening hours. Anyway, the foolish five go off to buy some oil and guess what, the bridegroom arrives when they are not there. Have you ever been out somewhere hurrying to run a quick errand, when your expected guests arrive at your home and you're not there? I imagine that we have probably all done that at some point too, or is it just me? The wise five who have made themselves ready through the right preparation, go straight into the wedding banquet. But then the door gets shut. Are we ready? Will the door be shut on us? I'd suggest not, if we are born again and we are therefore in the Kingdom of Heaven, but there is also a call for us in the Kingdom to be prepared. This is not only about being at the end time wedding feast, but it is also about how we are supposed to operate in the Kingdom today. If you want to be an Olympic athlete then you have to train to become highly efficient and effective at your sport. How is your spiritual training going? Prayer, Bible reading and fellowship with God by being in his presence, in other words, regularly worshipping and getting to know God more and more – these are some of your key exercises. This is how we train ourselves spiritually. You can be in the Kingdom but still be completely unprepared. If we as the Church want to build an army of prayer warriors and spiritually alert disciples, then that means each of us asking ourselves honestly – how am I doing? How prepared am I? (Matt. 25:8-10).

The foolish five turn up and want to get into the wedding banquet but they find that the door is shut and they ask for it to be opened. The reply comes… *"Truly I tell you, I don't **know** you"*. If this sounds familiar, then you have probably heard this before somewhere. It is that text about being true and false disciples (Matt. 7:23). Knowing God is therefore crucial, but it is not an intellectual knowledge of facts about God, rather it is a personal knowing and a two-way relational connection with God. Jesus finishes by telling the disciples to keep watch because they and we, like the ten virgins, have no idea when Jesus will return. So be ready Church – be ready (Matt. 25:11-13).

In Conclusion

Some of us today are well prepared, some are less prepared and some are unprepared. Which one are you?

What differentiates the foolish and the wise, is simply not being prepared. It will take effort from each of us to make ourselves ready. The Kingdom requires that you prepare and are ready spiritually for any eventuality.

When the final day comes each person will have to account for themselves and themselves alone. So don't be foolish with your spiritual life, while you are here on this earth. Let's not through thoughtlessness, or laziness, or irresponsibility, discharge our spiritual preparedness.

Here are some ways to help you to prepare spiritually:
- Take ownership and responsibility for your own walk with God.

- Use spiritual disciplines like prayer, solitude, worship, reading the word, in creative ways to connect personally with God every day.
- Learn to hear the voice of God more accurately by making time to be still, by listening to your spontaneous thoughts, pictures or visions and by journaling your conversation with God (Hab. 2:1-3).
- Commit to small groups to learn from and with others.
- Activate spiritual gifts and use the anointing that you were sealed with when you entered the Kingdom (2 Cor. 1:21-22).
- Be at your church prayer meetings.
- Start making disciples of others, by sharing your life experiences and what God has done in you and through you.

We as disciples of Jesus, are to be a people who walk in step with the Holy Spirit, day in day out, moment by moment. This is what it means to be prepared.

CHAPTER TWELVE

Talents

We move now to the twelfth and final "the Kingdom of Heaven is like" parable in Matthew: the parable of the talents.

What are you good at?

We are all good at something. Perhaps for you it is sport or painting, business, teaching, nursing, engineering, gardening, cooking or crafts. This list could go on. The truth is though, that we are all good at something, even if that something is not always highly valued by others or even appreciated the way it should be. We treat people like superstars but forget the single mum doing her very best. People are paid millions each year to entertain, while those saving lives in hospitals often struggle to make ends meet. Our world has things the wrong way up! We see in the Bible that God is the giver of good gifts to people (Matt. 7:11). I don't believe that God leaves people out.

Natural talent and hard work

I have always loved running. As a youngster, I even managed to race cross country at county level on a couple of occasions. I ran road and track as well, running a two hour forty-seven minute marathon and a four minute thirty second mile. I trained hard and had some talent, but others seemed to turn up to training and races and could just run so much faster. They just had a greater natural ability than I did. That didn't always seem fair. However, a combination of these things, natural talent and hard work, makes for an incredible resource in any field. In sport, they bring the ability to make champions; in industry, they take inventions into useable products; in science, they take experiments into health cures and vaccines; in literature, they give us great books; in art, they give us masterpieces; and in music, they give us incredible sounds and song.

Those who make it to these great heights of accomplishment are talented naturally, but work hard on their giftings as well. However, they could never have made it without the support, help, training and encouragement from many others, from people around them who will never become a household name. Whoever finds a vaccine or cure for cancer, or the current Covid-19 virus, will most likely end up famous, but it takes thousands of ordinary less talented people to give the treatments and vaccines to sick people.

So, we cannot all be the superstars and perhaps rich and famous. In reality we won't be. That does not matter, as long as we play our part, wherever God has placed us and wherever he will place us. He knows exactly what talents he has given us, and how he can enhance those with spiritual gifts and insight as well. We should never be negative to someone who is doing well with the talents they have been given. Instead, we should encourage and support them. We should also not compare ourselves and think that either they don't have much talent, or that they have more talent than I do. Simply discover the talent that God has given you and then begin to use it... *"in Christ we, though many, form one body, and each member belongs to all the others. ⁶ We have different gifts, according to the grace given to each of us. If your gift is prophesying, then prophesy in accordance with your faith; ⁷ if it is serving, then serve; if it is teaching, then teach;*

⁸ if it is to encourage, then give encouragement; if it is giving, then give generously; if it is to lead, do it diligently; if it is to show mercy, do it cheerfully (Rom. 12:5-8).

The Parable of the Talents

It is to drive home the point to his disciples of **being ready**, that Jesus then uses the two parables of the ten virgins and the talents in chapter twenty-five. The disciples need to know why they should be constantly alert, but while waiting for the unknown time of Jesus' promised return, they are to remain **faithful stewards**.

After the parable of the ten virgins comes the parable of the talents which is not about money. It is about Jesus being a harvester, who is asking us all to work in the harvest field, regardless of our level of ability. Whether you have five talents, two talents or only one talent…are you using what you have to help advance the Kingdom?

In this parable we see four main sections: 1) the distribution of resources, 2) the stewardship of resources, 3) the reward for good stewardship, and 4) laziness punished.

Distribution of Resources

*"Again, **it** will be like a man going on a journey, who called his servants and entrusted his wealth to them. ¹⁵ To one he gave five bags of gold, to another two bags, and to another one bag, each*

according to his ability. Then he went on his journey" (Matt. 25:14-15).

The term 'Kingdom of Heaven' is not actually mentioned in the original Greek, so here the NIV translates using 'it', where 'it' refers to the Kingdom of Heaven that was mentioned back in the previous parable (of the ten virgins), that comes immediately prior. In other translations like the New King James, the 'it' is replaced with exactly what the 'it' is referring to i.e. the Kingdom of Heaven.

The man was probably a businessman, who goes on a journey and entrusts his money to three servants according to their ability. It is worth noting that in this ancient culture, servants would have been given responsible functions and expected to look after many things.

One servant receives five talents, one receives two talents and one receives one talent. A talent is six-thousand denarii or six-thousand days of work, or about twenty years' salary. If we earn, for example, the UK average salary of £35k then one talent would equate to about £700,000! So, the one with two talents gets £1.4M and the other with five talents gets £3.5M. This symbolises a great privilege for what we have been afforded, even if we only have just one talent.

Stewardship of Resources

"The man who had received five bags of gold went at once and put his money to work and gained five bags more. [17] So also, the one with two bags of gold gained two more. [18] But the man who

had received one bag went off, dug a hole in the ground and hid his master's money" (Matt. 25:16-18).

The first two servants do business of some sort, we are not told exactly what, but they end up making 100% profit. The third servant ignores his instructions and just buries his talent in the ground. Back around that time in history, treasure was often hidden in the earth as a simple and effective place to keep money safe.

Reward for Good Stewardship

"After a long time the master of those servants returned and settled accounts with them. [20] The man who had received five bags of gold brought the other five. 'Master,' he said, 'you entrusted me with five bags of gold. See, I have gained five more.'
[21] "His master replied, 'Well done, good and faithful servant! You have been faithful with a few things; I will put you in charge of many things. Come and share your master's happiness!' [22] "The man with two bags of gold also came. 'Master,' he said, 'you entrusted me with two bags of gold; see, I have gained two more.'
[23] "His master replied, 'Well done, good and faithful servant! You have been faithful with a few things; I will put you in charge of many things. Come and share your master's happiness!'"'" (Matt. 25:19-23).

The master returns after his long trip. We don't know where and how far he actually went, but when he arrives, he calls the servants to account. This is a picture of when Jesus returns for his Church, and his calling of us to account for what we have done with the talent entrusted to us in this life. The first two servants give good account, that they both made a 100% profit.

These servants can be trusted and given more, and they share happiness with their master, perhaps like a modern-day share bonus scheme from your employer.

Will you and I be described as 'good and faithful' servants? If we use our talents well, then God will give us a greater sphere of influence and a greater scope of work. Both in this present Kingdom of Heaven and also when it comes in its future fullness. While we can see that people may not all be equal in talent, they should be equal in diligence and effort. Both servants receive the same commendation and the same reward.

Laziness is Punished

"Then the man who had received one bag of gold came. 'Master,' he said, 'I knew that you are a hard man, harvesting where you have not sown and gathering where you have not scattered seed. ²⁵ So I was afraid and went out and hid your gold in the ground. See, here is what belongs to you.' ²⁶ "His master replied, 'You wicked, lazy servant! So you knew that I harvest where I have not sown and gather where I have not scattered seed? ²⁷ Well then, you should have put my money on deposit with the bankers, so that when I returned I would have received it back with interest. ²⁸ "'So take the bag of gold from him and give it to the one who has ten bags. ²⁹ For whoever has will be given more, and they will have an abundance. Whoever does not have, even what they have will be taken from them. ³⁰ And throw that worthless servant outside, into the darkness, where there will be weeping and gnashing of teeth'"' (Matt. 25:24-30).

The third servant is treated very differently. He did not use his talent out of fear, earning 0% profit. He then tries to justify his actions, or should I say, lack of action! If you were loaned and given charge of £700,000 for a business owner or company, you would be expected to do something to increase it. Put yourself in the shoes of the master for a moment, if that was your money, you would expect something back too – wouldn't you.

Fear meant that the money was not even invested, which was easy enough to do. That would at least have been something. I wonder how many times we as disciples of Jesus, have missed opportunities to use our talent because of fear. 'Do not fear' is the most used phase in the Bible and is still applicable to us today. Love drives out fear and God is love (1 John 4). If we walk closely with Jesus, his love is able to cast out our fear, and we are better placed to be able to do as he instructs.

"Lazy and wicked". These are harsh words indeed. The servant was right about one thing. the potential harshness of the master's response. Too lazy to trade and even too lazy to take it to the bank, to place the money on deposit and gain at least a little interest. The lazy servant loses his only talent and it is given to the first servant, who now has, an abundance of eleven talents or £7.7M.

The lazy servant is severely punished and thrown out of the Kingdom of Heaven. Yes, this does seem severe, but we have to ask if the third servant was even a disciple at all. The kind of behaviour he exhibits is not compatible with being a disciple of Jesus. But let's not lose sight of how generous the master has been with the first two servants. God is generous but he is also just.

As disciples, we have been equipped to serve Jesus and to extend the influence of his rule and reign over this earth. All of us will be called to account for the stewardship of our own abilities, not for anyone else's.

Observations

Those that have done nothing with their faith are not disciples of Jesus after all, and they will be condemned. I don't think arriving at a church building every week for an hour counts for much. There are many who 'go to church' but they don't know Jesus personally. Those who go out of a sense of religious duty or even just for entertainment won't 'cut the mustard'. We have to know Jesus by inviting him into our lives, and that should transform us allowing us to know him personally. Then, additionally, we need to begin to do something with the talents he has given us.

We do need to spend our time here on earth wisely. Any unused gifts are lost opportunities. We freely enter the Kingdom of Heaven, but then we are supposed to stay connected to our King Jesus, and work for him in extending it. We will be rewarded according to our efforts. God has given you gifts, abilities, connections and opportunities, are you using them wisely and diligently…

Two used their talents profitably – one did not.

Two are congratulated – one is not.

Two share their masters delight – one does not.

Does Jesus mean very much to you? Does his Kingdom mean anything to you? If you bury what he has given you, it does seem as if you don't really care about what he has given you.

The lazy servant treated what he was given as though it was dead, and he broke the trust given him. We cannot act like this and expect to be part of a Kingdom that does not behave this way. Do you care about your spiritual life and your walk with God? If you do, then you will do something with the talents you have.

In Conclusion

What are you talented at? The talents you have need to be used. For example, in playing the piano or golf, if you don't practise you will get very rusty very quickly.

The parable of the talents is not about money and it is not about how much talent we have. We all have some talent, but what are we doing with ours? Jesus has entrusted us with his Kingdom, are we investing in it and helping it to grow?

The two faithful servants knew their responsibility, did their job diligently, and they were rewarded for their faithfulness. The Kingdom requires that you be a **faithful worker.**

How are you activating your talents? One talent was plenty. Are you being dependable with your resource? The one talent mentality keeps things are they were, with no investment, no development, no change and no growth! One did not even try. Trying and failing is better than not trying at all. What can I do? What difference can I make? I have nothing or so very little to give or offer. Remember the two loaves and five fishes that Jesus used the disciples to feed five-thousand. Your every little helps the common good. **Your talent is needed**.

SECTION THREE

Additional Kingdom Concepts

CHAPTER ONE

Further Kingdom Concepts

We have now looked at all twelve of the "Kingdom of Heaven is like" statements in Matthew's Gospel. Isn't it interesting that there happen to be twelve 'like' statements, following the pattern of twelve tribes of Israel (OT) and the twelve disciples (NT)? I do hope you are beginning to see something of the Territory of this spiritual Kingdom, its areas of operation, and how one should function in it. We are going to now look at some further **Kingdom** concepts that we find in Matthew.

Childlikeness

There are a few times that the Kingdom of Heaven is compared to children…

*"At that time the disciples came to Jesus and asked, '**Who, then, is the greatest in the kingdom of heaven?**' He called a little child to him, and placed the child among them"* (Matt. 18:1-2).

*"And he said: '**Truly I tell you, unless you change and become like little children, you will never enter the kingdom of heaven.**⁴ Therefore, whoever takes the lowly position of this child is the greatest in the kingdom of heaven'"* (Matt. 18:3-4).

*"Jesus said, 'Let the little children come to me, and do not hinder them, for **the kingdom of heaven belongs to such as these**'"* (Matt. 19:14).

Have you seen the news stories of when politicians are running for office, and want to appear that they are a super caring 'people person'? They have video footage taken with them helping little children and then use this as a means of self-promotion. Well, Jesus didn't do this to make himself look good – he had no need for that – but instead he provides a very real demonstration of some boundaries in living from a Kingdom perspective.

The context here is the disciples talking with Jesus and asking him about greatness in the Kingdom. Jesus uses a child to demonstrate greatness in an upside-down Kingdom, where the last shall be first and the weakest and most vulnerable will lead. I believe this is because they hold the right qualities of faith, trust, innocence, purity and obedience, as examples.

Unless we change and I mean really change, both as adults and as young people (in Israel at that time a twelve-year-old was considered an adult that would start their working career), we may not even enter the Kingdom, let alone become either experts or great within it. All of us really must **change**!

We must learn to lay aside all of our pride in our intellect and our strong opinions, and become pure and innocent like children. Being born again is what gets us in, but we really must only see that as a starting point in a life-long journey into both holiness and childlike qualities, which essentially describes the sanctification process. It is only because of the amazing grace of Jesus that he accepts us as we are, warts and all, but he wants us to take very seriously our becoming ever more innocent of evil (Rom. 16:19).

Therefore, the more like children we become in purity, in holiness, trust and obedience, then the greater we become, but this is not a hierarchical position in order to gain a rank or position. No, I don't believe that is what scripture means. Rather, innocent children usually obey what their parents say and so we change by becoming innocent and trusting of our heavenly Father – so much so that we obey him in everything.

Greatness

*"'What is it you want?' he asked. She said, 'Grant that one of these two sons of mine **may sit at your right and the other at your left in your kingdom**'"* (Matt. 20:21). We touched on this briefly at the start of the chapter on the parable of the wedding feast. Here is Jesus answer in full... *"You don't know what you are asking,"* Jesus said to them. *"Can you drink the cup I am going to drink?"* *"We can,"* they answered. Jesus said to them, *"You will indeed drink from my cup, but to sit at my right or left is not for me to grant. These places belong to those for whom they have been prepared by my Father."* When the ten heard about this, they were indignant with the two brothers. Jesus called them together and said, *"You know that the rulers of the Gentiles lord it over them, and their high officials exercise authority over them. Not so with you. Instead, whoever wants to become great among you must be your servant, and whoever wants to be first must be your slave—just as the Son of Man did not come to be served, but to serve, and to give his life as a ransom for many""* (Matt. 20:22-28).

In the Kingdom, there is true equality regardless of age, race, educational achievement, class, culture and gender. We miss the point **if we ask** to be great in this Kingdom because that is us seeking status. We need to seek Jesus to become like him, to seek the Father that Jesus opened up the way for us to access, obey what Papa says, and also to seek the Holy Spirit who empowers us to do the work of this spiritual Kingdom. Leave the work of the Father to the Father because God is more than capable; he knows what he is doing and will have heaven arranged as he pleases. Our role is to hear and obey him.

Have you ever felt bypassed for a promotion? We can feel very upset, agitated and think that life is not fair. Well, this certainly also upset the rest of the disciples when it was requested. They become indignant – they are very cross and upset. If we keep seeking promotion in the Kingdom then we will upset others whether we mean to or not. My advice is to let God do the promoting and focus on being a servant to others, just as Jesus did.

Eunuchs

*"For there are eunuchs who were born that way, and there are eunuchs who have been made eunuchs by others – **and there are those who choose to live like eunuchs for the sake of the kingdom of heaven**. The one who can accept this should accept it"* (Matt. 19:12).

I'm also no scientist, so I had to look up a definition of what a eunuch is biologically i.e. if they are 'born that way'. This was the most helpful definition that I found, because I could at least understand the ending… *"when there is nondisjunction of the sex chromosomes during gamete formation resulting in XXY as their sex chromosomes, thus they are neither completely males nor females"*. Eunuchs 'made by others', would be those who have gone through male castration. Then there is another category of people 'choosing to live like' a eunuch, for the sake of the Kingdom.

The way God made people is with strong desires and needs. After the desire for food and shelter, one of the next strongest desires is for sexual intimacy with another. This is something a eunuch cannot have, but they can certainly still love people and be loved, but without that physical intimacy. The Kingdom is so important that for some they will choose to live a life of celibacy, which removes that sexual intimacy but not the ability to love or be loved. Notice that I did not say 'singleness', because in singleness people can still choose to be sexually intimate with others, even though that is not what God recommends. In singleness, one still has to choose to live for the Kingdom of Heaven, without yielding to this strong desire, which is so very difficult. The point is that the Kingdom is so important; we should be willing to put it ahead of even **our strongest desires**.

Woes

"Woe to you, teachers of the law and Pharisees, you hypocrites! ***You shut the door of the kingdom of heaven in people's faces.*** *You yourselves do not enter, nor will you let those enter who are trying to"* (Matt. 23:13).

Here Jesus is teaching in Jerusalem before his crucifixion, and he challenges the religious leaders of the day with his seven woes. One of the woes in particular mentions the Kingdom and the fact that religion, in and of itself, shuts the door to it. Those who do teach these religious ways and laws, without the relationship to the one who made them (and was standing right before them), actually prevent other people from entering the Kingdom. *"You yourselves do not enter"* – notice that knowing facts about a book or even laws in the Bible, will not get you into the Kingdom of Heaven. The thing that upset Jesus the most, was the fact that their ways stopped others from entering.

People may be willing and wanting and trying to get into a relationship with God, and we as the Church must not put a bunch of rules and regulations in front of them. We should not create barriers that they stumble to get over. We must do the exact opposite, inviting people into the Kingdom, by pointing them to Jesus and giving them what we have freely received, to bring them into relationship with Father, Son and Holy Spirit. People are to be made to feel as though they belong with us, even before they believe. The love that Christians show for each other, in a place that welcomes the presence of the Holy Spirit, will enable others to believe for themselves (John 13:35).

Where preached

"Nation will rise against nation, and kingdom against kingdom. There will be famines and earthquakes in various places" (Matt. 24:7). *"And this gospel of the kingdom will be preached in the whole world as a testimony to all nations, and then the end will come"* (Matt. 24:14).

In chapter twenty-four Jesus depicts the end of this world as we know it, and what will happen when he returns. We already see, in many parts of this world, nation at war with nation and kingdom against kingdom. The gospel story, the good news of Jesus Christ as Lord of all and Saviour to those who choose to accept and follow him, will be preached to all nations. Again, this text helps us to see that the territory of the Kingdom of Heaven is the whole world and everything in it, both good and bad.

Our call is to know Jesus, who then sends us out into all the world. For us today, that means spreading the message of Jesus, that we freely received, to those who have not yet heard. This means people in our locality and sphere of influence, as well as those in other nations – on mission both at home and overseas.

Prepared

*"Then the King will say to those on his right, "Come, you who are blessed by my Father; take your inheritance, the **kingdom prepared for you since the creation of the world**""* (Matt. 25:34).

When we as the sheep are separated to the right, which happens to those following Jesus, he will say come and take your inheritance, because you are blessed by the Father. What will you inherit? The Kingdom! This is why we need to practise living its ways now, so it is not foreign to us when it arrives in its fullness. We will see it, in its fullness and majesty, and we will live with the King. In the meantime, **heaven can exist on earth now**. It is most certainly worth living in now and it will be so much more wonderful then. God has planned this for you, since he created not just you, but since he created the world. God is a pretty good planner and knows exactly which ones he has for your life (Jer. 29:11).

In Conclusion

These 'further' Kingdom concepts in Matthew should also be important to us as disciples:

Childlikeness: to welcome and grow in purity, trust and faith, as well as in obedience.

Greatness: to serve Jesus humbly and not for personal status, and without using self-promotion.

Eunuchs: to prefer the Kingdom to even our strongest desires.

Woes: not to place barriers in people's way but instead invite people into relationship with Jesus.

Where preached: to take the gospel to the whole world that we are sent in to.

Already prepared: to recognise that the Kingdom has awaited you a very long time, so learn to live in it now.

Did you notice that much of this is about your character development? In what ways can you start to do something different in each of these areas of your life? They will help you grow as a disciple if you commit yourself to them.

CHAPTER TWO

The Keys of the Kingdom

I hope as we have journeyed together for a while now, that you are beginning to see more clearly the of the territory of this incredible and very real spiritual Kingdom. Having now covered the relevant parables and Kingdom statements in Matthew, next, we head back to chapter sixteen. Here we will look at the crucial **Keys** to the Kingdom. Even by just looking at the territory, let alone the other three components of citizens, laws and the King, we can see that Jesus left us with an abundance of information on his Kingdom. But what is its key? Can we unlock it?

Kingdom Keys

"When Jesus came to the region of Caesarea Philippi, he asked his disciples, "Who do people say the Son of Man is?" [14] They replied, "Some say John the Baptist; others say Elijah; and still others, Jeremiah or one of the prophets." [15] "But what about you?" he asked. "Who do you say I am?" [16] Simon Peter answered, "You are the Messiah, the Son of the living God." [17] Jesus replied, "Blessed are you, Simon son of Jonah, for this was not revealed to you by flesh and blood, but by my Father in heaven. [18] And I tell you that you are Peter, and on this rock I will build my church, and the gates of Hades will not overcome it. [19] I will give you the keys of the kingdom of heaven; whatever you bind on earth will be bound in heaven, and whatever you loose on earth will be loosed in heaven"" (Matt. 16:13-19).

Here we find that Jesus and the disciples had just fed the four-thousand, and they go by boat on the lake (or the sea of Galilee), to the vicinity of Magadan between Tiberias and Capernaum (Matt. 15:39). There Jesus is tested by both the Pharisees and Sadducees, who ask him for a sign. At the beginning of chapter sixteen, he simply points them to Jonah the prophet. Next they sail north, probably to Capernaum. When crossing on the boat Jesus warned the disciples about the teaching of the Pharisees and Sadducees. Back on dry land, they walk north approximately thirty-five miles (56km), a good two days walk in my book, to Caesarea Philippi.

Was Jesus a fitness freak? Why when he needed ultimately to get to Jerusalem in the South, would he walk for two whole days in the opposite direction? There must have been a very important lesson that he wanted to teach his disciples, both back then and therefore for us today. They arrive in the region of Caesarea Philippi and we are left wondering what must have been so special about this place? Well, Caesarea Philippi had become the centre of pagan religion. It sits at the foot of Mount Hermon, the highest mountain in Israel at over seven-thousand feet, and which is mentioned on numerous occasions in the OT. This mountain is high enough for snow in the winter months, which melts and makes its way down through the limestone rock, into two pools of water. Apparently, these pools contain seventy-two natural springs, which is a number I like as Jesus sent out seventy-two disciples (Luke 10:1). These pools of water are the headwater of the river Jordan, which is probably the Bible's most significant river. You may well remember: that it separated when Israel crossed over into the promised land, when Elijah crossed over, and also that Jesus was baptised in it. Whilst this area seemed an important source and significant place, faithful Jews would never visit and we will soon discover why!

Jesus introduces his very important lesson with a question… *"Who do people say the Son of Man is?"* This is to get the disciples to think about who Jesus really is. Their reply is certainly an impressive list of great people to be compared to: John the Baptist, Elijah, Jeremiah or one of the prophets. We wouldn't mind being compared to the likes of these, would we. In their answer, they include a forerunner to the Messiah, someone who did not taste death, and a spokesman of God. But Jesus is so much more than these! But now comes the real question, and it is personal to each of the disciples back then and for us now… *"**But what about you?**"* he asked. *"**Who do you say I am?**"* Jesus knew exactly who he was, but did they, and do we? Jesus is making this personal. We have to answer the question individually. What is **your** answer? The bold and outspoken disciple Peter jumps in as usual… *"You are the Messiah, the Son of the living God"*. He's got it! The first public recognition and declaration that Jesus is the Messiah, the anointed one and the saviour of mankind. As you can imagine Jesus is rather pleased with his answer… *"Blessed are you, Simon son of Jonah, for this was not revealed to you by flesh and blood, but by my Father in heaven"*. The reason I believe Jesus was so pleased, is because for the first time one of the disciples is hearing the Father speak. Peter is receiving heavenly revelation and wisdom. Jesus continues… *"And I tell you that you are Peter, and on this rock I will build my church **[ekklesia]**, and the **gates of Hades** will not overcome it"*.

I think it will be most helpful if we look first at the gates of Hades and then the *ekklesia*.

The Gates of Hades

At the foot of Mount Hermon is a very large rock face, with a deep cave that would fill with water. Around 200BC in the Hellenistic era, Greek goat shepherds settled into the area of Caesarea Philippi and used the two pools, with the seventy-two springs mentioned earlier, to water their goats. A town nearby became established. The Greek goat shepherds lived in a rural setting by the caves rather than in the town. Their rural location was a very dark place spiritually, because there they worshipped the Greek god of Pan. This pagan religion believed that the cave was itself the frightful door to the great abyss – the entrance to the underworld – the very gates of Hades.

Pantheism is derived from two Greek words, *pan* meaning 'all', or 'of everything', and *theos* meaning 'god' or 'divine'. When combined, they mean the god of everything in nature. Perhaps because of his association with nature and animals, Pan did not have the appearance of a normal man. The bottom half of his body was like a goat, with the top half of his body being human. Pan is often depicted with horns on his head, an abnormally large male organ and a very unattractive face. He is not one of the major gods of Ancient Greece, but he is one of most often referenced figures in Greek mythology, and considered to be one of the oldest Greek gods. Pan ruled over shepherds, hunters, and rustic music and he possessed enormous strength. He could also run for long periods and would never be injured. He could transform objects into different forms and was able to teleport himself from earth to Mount Olympus and back. In an old tale of war, Pan helps a friend survive by letting out an immense cry that frightened the enemy, who then fled. From this legend, we get the word 'panic', the sudden uncontrollable fear that leads people into irrational behaviour. Pan would go into the nearby towns and villages at night, to frighten the people and protect the shepherds and the goats. People were terrified of the cave below Mount Hermon because it was the place where Pan lived.

The worship of Pan began in rural areas far from the populated towns, so large temples were not built. This worship was centred in nature, often in caves or grottos. Festivals were held each year, at which people would have to buy goats in the town's market, then celebrate by dancing with them or even abusing them. They would take the goats to the cave where they were slaughtered and thrown into the water as an offering to appease Pan. If their goat floated on the water, they would have to repeat the process, until their next goat sank. The water in the cave became red with goats' blood and so this cave became known as the gates of Hades. Hades means the unseen world of departed spirits. This was seen literally as a portal into hell itself. No wonder, that God-fearing Jews would not go there!

Ekklesia

Jesus used the words "on this rock" to describe Peter. Catholics generally believe that this means that Jesus gave Peter the keys to his Kingdom, to in effect say who can enter the Kingdom. Peter went on to become the Bishop of Rome or Pope, and this honour is passed down to each Bishop of Rome thereafter. Protestants more often believe that this means that it is through the Church itself that Jesus will build his Kingdom. I don't believe that the rock is either the Pope or the Church, but rather it refers to God himself. We do see this elsewhere in scripture... *"**The Lord is my rock**, my fortress and my deliverer; **my God is my rock**, in whom I take refuge"* (2 Sam. 22:2-3). Also, Jesus is presented as the cornerstone (Eph. 2:20).

It is not upon Peter, a mere man, nor upon the church establishment with all of its buildings and structure, that the Kingdom will be built. The rock, I believe, refers to Jesus' Messiahship which Peter had just confessed through divine revelation. That alone will be the basis for Jesus to extend his Kingdom and build his Church. Usually, the Greek word *ekklesia* is translated by our word 'church', but it actually means those who are set apart, the gathered saints, or people who recognise the sonship of Jesus. This has nothing to do with physical church buildings.

It is important to remember that the Kingdom of Heaven is a spiritual Kingdom. The Church is often referred to in scripture as the 'Bride of Christ', which portrays both an intimate and personal relationship with Jesus. The disciples of Jesus remain in union with him, as they live out their lives for him. Briggs helpfully describes the ekklesia and here is my paraphrased version: ekklesia is the **governmental authority and rulership of a heavenly outpost of divine legislation**; to advance the Kingdom, **through the indispensable means of prayer**.[12]

---

[12] Briggs, D. *Ekklesia Rising. The Authority of Christ in Communities of Contending Prayer* (Kansas: Champion Press, 2014).

Do you see your true significance as a disciple of Jesus, as part of the ekklesia? Do you understand your role in extending this spiritual Kingdom? I guess this is why I believe that prayer should be consumed with passion. We should be a **people passionate about prayer, who pray passionately**. The disciples back then, and we today, do not need to fear, because even Hades itself will not be able to overcome the praying saints! We are supposed to make up the spiritual government of this spiritual Kingdom, to take down the works of our spiritual enemy. How is it possible that we don't see prayer as the most important gathered meeting for us to be at? We must seek the King's wisdom and revelation so we can act out our governmental position in the spiritual realm, as the ruling council or supreme court. The ekklesia needs to understand its identity and its calling, as this is what God builds up, to defeat the demonic spiritual forces which otherwise keep our communities lost and bound.

Notice that Jesus doesn't give us the keys to the Church, although some of us do hold keys to our physical church buildings… *"I will give you the keys of the kingdom of heaven"*. Instead, he gives us the keys to the Kingdom of Heaven. You will also perhaps notice that 'keys' is plural, which means that we as disciples each have one. Jesus has given us an astonishing amount of information on the Kingdom of Heaven throughout Matthew. A bit like the information needed to design and build a car. But when a car is finally made, to make it start you have to **have the key.** Even then, that is not enough to make the car move anywhere. Owning a key is vital, but so is the other necessary fact, that you actually have to **use the key**.

The key is our authority to make this spiritual Kingdom advance. It is the thing that **unlocks heaven on earth: prayer!** *"Whatever you bind on earth will be bound in heaven, and whatever you loose on earth will be loosed in heaven"*. To bind means what you forbid and loose means what you permit.

In Conclusion

Jesus goes a long way, out of his way, to take the disciples to a place of significant darkness. A place full of demons that Rabbis detested. At the Gates of Hades, there is an important lesson for the ekklesia, for all professing and active followers of Jesus. Namely that two things happen: firstly, a truly profound understanding of who Jesus is and, secondly, a truly profound declaration of the spiritual authority given by Jesus to his disciples.

When we have a revelation of the true all-surpassing authority of Jesus and that he gives this authority to us, surely it should make all the difference to how we see ourselves on this earth. Jesus incredibly confers on us a Kingdom that his Father conferred on him… *"I confer on you a kingdom, just as my Father conferred one on me"* (Luke 22:29). This realisation must lead us triumphantly into the prayer room, to battle for our communities, our nation and the nations of the world.

Jesus has given a massive amount of detail about his Kingdom, but here he gives us the key to it all…our prayers that will overcome the dark spiritual kingdoms of this world. If we don't exercise this authority given to us, we and our homes, our community, our nation and our world will continually be hampered beyond need.

If we want to build up our local ekklesia and extend its reach, then we have the authority to do so through living a life of passionate prayer. We have to be in step with the Holy Spirit through our praying, listening and obeying his promptings, moment by moment. If we know who Jesus really is and who we really are as his disciples, then we will exercise our spiritual authority in prayer.

Here is your key. The question is…will you use it?

CHAPTER THREE

A Borderless Kingdom

In this present age, that is, between the age when Jesus was incarnate on earth and the time of his return, we live in a Kingdom that has no borders, yet transcends our entire world. This is extremely significant. I'll come back to why this is so.

This world is set in a series of continents that contain many nations, each having its own border to define its own land territory. Crossing national borders will nearly always require identification like a passport or ID card. Then within a nation, we find regions or states or counties that are also bordered, but with free movement. Then there are cities, towns and villages, which are also, all bordered. We border our neighbourhoods, our streets and even our properties. Unfortunately, we fight over these borders at every level, from the garden fence dispute, to gang warfare, to civil or national wars, to international wars that can even be worldwide.

The kingdoms of this world and their governmental systems and structures generally tend to divide the people that live in them. This can be through all kinds of things like political association, race, social status, education, favoured sports teams, musical preference, etc. Humanity is a bordered people that are also very often divided.

Jesus ushered in a new borderless and spiritual Kingdom that anyone can enter (God foreknows who will), and he prayed that we would be one... *"my prayer is not for them [the disciples] alone. I pray also for those who will believe in me through their message, that all of them may be one, Father, just as you are in me and I am in you"* (John 17:20-21). One people group that follows Jesus is united on mission to reach every other group on this planet, regardless of how different to us they might be.

Imagine a world with no land boundaries, no political divide, no corruption or greed, no racial or gender prejudice, no cultural or educational divide, no ageism, no social status or class divide, no struggle for power, no sectarianism – no 'I'm better than you!' **Jesus ushered in one Kingdom, across one planet earth, for one race – the human race**. This is why when disciples of Jesus travel to distant places around the world and meet other disciples, there is an immediate connection. Although different in almost every way, we are of the same borderless Kingdom, representing the same wonderful King.

This is the Kingdom we now live in and which shapes us to be more like itself, than like the kingdoms of this world. Do you see the significance of what we offer? Who would not want to join? The challenge we all face as Christians, though, is to authentically live this way as individuals, so that our churches can be the places of hope and light that they are meant to be.

When the future Kingdom arrives in all its fullness, with Jesus' return to this earth and his long reign, only one border will be put in place or imposed for humanity. This is the eternal and uncrossable divide between heaven and hell.

It is important for us therefore to look at these two often confusing and difficult subjects from a Kingdom perspective too. Doing so will give us a broader view and understanding of the territory of the future Kingdom, and its impact for us today in the present Kingdom, further motivating us to share the good news of Jesus.

CHAPTER FOUR

The Reality of Hell

The doctrine of hell can be a difficult one to understand and to speak about. Let's face it, many of us are either uncomfortable talking about hell or are confused and uncertain about it. A lot of churches avoid the subject altogether. But that is not helpful for us as disciples who are trying to understand the territory of the Kingdom. Where does hell fit in exactly and why is it important?

What we understand about hell, does shape our view of the importance of the gospel message of the Kingdom of Heaven. If we don't accept hell as a reality, then we won't see the urgent need for us to be disciples on a mission.

Why Hell?

God is a Holy God and must be separate from sin. Because Adam's original sin brought sin like a disease into our world, we are all guilty of it or infected by it, and fall short of God's holy standard and glory (Rom. 3:23). We all therefore deserve God's eternal punishment, which is a separation from him. Hell is mankind's default destination and we need a saviour from sin, or we stand condemned. We can stay in this state of depravity and be eternally punished, or we can enter into a loving relationship with God through his son Jesus. We can turn from our sin and choose to willingly submit to the

Saviour Jesus and accept his free gift of salvation; his perfect sacrifice for our sin.

What did Jesus say about Hell?

Jesus talked about hell more than any other person in the Bible. He makes reference to hell and describes it with great imagery. Jesus describes it as a place of *eternal torment* (Luke 16:23); of *unquenchable fire and where the worm does not die* (Mark 9:48); *where people will weep and gnash their teeth* (Matt. 13:42); he calls hell a place of *outer darkness* (Matt. 8:12; 25:30); and *from which there is no return over a great chasm, even to warn loved ones* (Luke 16:19-31).

In Luke chapter sixteen, Jesus depicts a wicked man suffering fiery torment in hades, contrasted with another in the bosom of Abraham, which represents eternal comfort. On both sides, they could talk, think, remember, feel and care. Jesus explains, though, that it is impossible to cross over from one to the other. There is no need, therefore, to pray for the dead as their position cannot be changed. This also corresponds to the Ancient Jewish belief in *hades* or *sheol*, that it contained separate divisions for the wicked and righteous. It is clear that Jesus both understood and warned us concerning the absolute reality of hell.

Different Biblical words for Hell

In the OT, the Hebrew word **sheol** is the term used to describe 'the grave' or 'death'.
In the NT, the Greek word **hades** occurs nine times and means a place of torment or the abode of the dead.

These two terms, both *sheol* and *hades*, can be viewed as synonymous. It is generally agreed that they do not typically refer to the place of 'eternal punishment', but to the grave, the temporary abode of the dead or the underworld.

Next in the NT, the Greek word **gehenna** occurs twelve times and is always translated as either "Hell" or "Hellfire", which refers to the 'eternal destination' of the wicked. Perhaps a modern-day image to help us, would be the horrendous and unprecedented Australian bush fires of 2019. In Matthew chapter ten, Jesus compares hell to a physical place Hinnom. Gehenna comes from the Hebrew *ge* which means land or valley and *Hinnom*, which was a dump outside the walls of Jerusalem, where offal and rubbish were continuously burned and represented eternal torment. Originally gehenna referred to the Ben Hinnom Valley south-west of Jerusalem. This is the place where, centuries earlier, children were sacrificed in the fire by those worshipping the god Molek (2 Kings 23:10), so it was a despised region.

There is one other NT Greek word **tartarus** that only occurs once in 2 Peter 2:4. This refers to a subterranean place of divine punishment lower than Hades.

Let's take a deeper look into how Jesus explained hell. In chapters twenty-four and twenty-five of Matthew, we see Jesus describing the signs of the end of the age. In this, he is saying: be watchful (Matt. 24:42) and be ready (Matt. 24:44), because the timing of his return is unknown. It is to drive home this point of **being ready** that Jesus then uses the parables of the ten virgins and the parable of the talents which is not about money, but about Jesus being a harvester asking us all to work in the harvest field, regardless of our level of ability. This is the background leading up to the story of the sheep and the goats, that brings home the reason why we need to be ready and faithful stewards.

Sheep and Goats

"When the Son of Man comes in his glory, and all the angels with him, he will sit on his glorious throne. *32* **All the nations will be gathered before him, and he will separate the people one from another as a shepherd separates the sheep from the goats**. *33* He will put the sheep on his right and the goats on his left. *34* "Then the King will say to those on his right, 'Come, you who are blessed by my Father; take your inheritance, the kingdom prepared for you since the creation of the world. *35* For I was hungry and you gave me something to eat, I was thirsty and you gave me something to drink, I was a stranger and you invited me in, *36* I needed clothes and you clothed me, I was sick and you looked after me, I was in prison and you came to visit me.'

37 "Then the righteous will answer him, 'Lord, when did we see you hungry and feed you, or thirsty and give you something to drink? *38* When did we see you a stranger and invite you in, or needing clothes and clothe you? *39* When did we see you sick or in prison and go to visit you?' *40* "The King will reply, 'Truly I tell you, whatever you did for one of the least of these brothers and sisters of mine, you did for me.' *41* "Then he will say to those on his left, '**Depart from me, you who are cursed, into the eternal fire prepared for the devil and his angels**. *42* For I was hungry and you gave me nothing to eat, I was thirsty and you gave me nothing to drink, *43* I was a stranger and you did not invite me in, I needed clothes and you did not clothe me, I was sick and in *prison and you did not look after me.'* [44] *"They also will answer, 'Lord, when did we see you hungry or thirsty or a stranger or needing clothes or sick or in prison, and did not help you?'* [45] *"He will reply, 'Truly I tell you, whatever you did not do for one of the least of these, you did not do for me.'* [46] *"**Then they will go away to eternal punishment, but the righteous to eternal life.**""* (Matt. 25:31-46).

I have highlighted a few of the verses in the text above, because I want to touch on them briefly now. At the end of history, everyone will be gathered before Jesus, where he will divide humanity into "sheep" and "goats". Some have thought this to mean a separation of those in the Church, that is, true from false believers. However, the text is clear that **all nations** will be gathered for judgment. If the territory of the Kingdom is in fact this entire world – then **all of humanity will be separated** into either the righteous (sheep) or the wicked (goats). The separation is stark: it's one or the other (Matt. 25:32). We see that the wicked are banished to "eternal fire". This is the place God created for the devil and his demons (which are fallen angels), but the wicked also join them there (Matt. 25:41). No one has yet been there, including Satan, as it will be populated on the final judgment day. Still, not a place you will find in your holiday brochure!

Fortunately, the righteous will go on to have eternal life in the Kingdom with God. The righteous are mentioned back in Matthew 5:20: unless their righteousness surpasses that of the Pharisees, they will certainly not enter the Kingdom of Heaven. Those who enter the Kingdom are those born of the Spirit. They are the ones who are blessed and also robed with Jesus' righteousness. It is by faith in Jesus alone that gives a person this right standing before God. Jesus does invite everyone to trust in him to receive eternal life rather than eternal punishment (John 3:16-18), but not all will accept his invitation (Matt. 25:46).

The Protestant View

The wider Protestant doctrine or view of hell uses the term of the 'intermediate state' to describe the time between physical death (or hades) and a person's resurrection for final judgement into eternal punishment (or gehenna).

The Westminster Confession of 1646 states... *"but the wicked, who know not God, and obey not the gospel of Jesus Christ, shall be cast into **eternal torments**, and punished with everlasting destruction from the presence of the Lord, and from the glory of his power"* (Chapter XXXIII, Of the Last Judgment). Hell will be a place of unending conscious torment, and an irrevocable eternal separation from God.

Further Thoughts

At death, unbelievers go to torment in hades, while believers go to paradise. These happen immediately and are known as the intermediate state.

Hades in the future is itself thrown into the "lake of fire", after being emptied of the dead (Rev. 20:13-15). It is the final destiny of every person who does not choose to receive God's free gift of salvation. People will be consigned there forever at the final judgment, and Jesus has its keys... *"I am the Living One; I was dead, and now look, I am alive for ever and ever! And I hold the keys of death and Hades"* (Rev 1:18).

Hell is an unspeakable, unending reality (John 3:18-20, 36) even if it is only described using symbols. Existence in hell is therefore impossible to know exactly, but there will be an eternal total absence of God. Life will be very disturbed and dominated by sin, and with a continual suffering of both body and soul. Hell is for God's just judgment against sin. It is not our job to judge other people and God's divine mercy will extend as far as possible, but there will be some surprises on judgement day (Matt 7:21-23).

We can see from what we have learnt that the following, sometimes common beliefs, are not true to scripture: 1) that the unbeliever is annihilated at death or people simply cease to exist [annihilation], 2) that all people will be saved and simply go to heaven [universalism], or 3) that those who believe will go from mortal to immortal, but those who don't believe are then punished depending on the sins or crimes they have committed [conditional immortality].

There are areas of debate around the fate of the un-evangelised (those who have never heard the gospel), including those who die in infancy, those living in remote places of the world and those who are mentally disabled. Augustine believed that people in these categories would be damned to hell because of original sin, while many others believe that our merciful God will make an exception in these cases.

When Jesus does return, the dead in Christ will rise first (1 Thes. 4:16), believers in paradise will be resurrected and believers alive on earth at that moment will meet him in the air. This is called the Rapture of the Church (1 Thes. 4:17). Both sets of believers will then rule with Christ on earth for one-thousand years (Rev. 20:1-6). After this millennial reign of Christ, there will be the final judgement. The unbelievers alive at that point, along with those in death and hades, will be delivered up and will be judged and forever join the devil and his angels in hell (Rev. 20:11-15). At this same point, believers will be with Jesus forever in the new heaven and new earth (Rev. 21:1-4). This puts me into the 'pre-millennial' theological category.

In Conclusion

The Bible, both OT and NT, teaches about life after death and a conscious existence after death (Isa. 14:9-11, 15-17; Matt. 22:31; Luke 16:19-31). When it uses the term 'sleep', this relates to the body only, as our soul cannot cease to exist.

Is what Jesus teaches about hell metaphorical or literal? Terms like darkness, weeping, gnashing of teeth and fire certainly are not positive descriptions. If they are only metaphorical then we know it is still going to be bad. If they are literal it's also very bad! Take a moment and try to think of this world that has both good and bad in it, and suddenly all of the good is no longer there. That too would be very bad. Whilst the righteous will be separated to be with God, the unrighteous will not be with God. They will make up a mass of unrighteous people, which could well be thought of as the worst kind of poverty.

Our curiosity about death and the afterlife are not completely satisfied, either by the biblical terminology or the wider verses themselves. God has indeed left us with enough to ponder over, without us having to be obsessed with how every detail might play out. What we do know is that either eternal torment in hell or eternal joy in heaven awaits everyone.

Death brings this irrevocable final destiny based entirely upon whether a person trusts in Jesus and his payment for their sin, and puts their faith in him. Therefore, **the gospel message remains urgent today!**

We will never fully understand all the mysteries involved, but with the stark reality of hell, we must be thankful to God for sending Jesus into our lives, and use this as the right motivation **to share him with others**.

CHAPTER FIVE

The Wonder of Heaven

The doctrine of heaven can also be difficult to understand. We know that heaven is good and hell is bad, and that there is life after death, as an eternal conscious state, where all of mankind will be separated into the sheep and goats (Matt. 25:31-46). The sheep are the righteous who go to paradise until Christ's return to earth. A key phrase "with the Lord/Christ", confirms where believers will go after death (Phil. 1:23; 1 Thes. 4:17; 2 Cor. 5:8). The goats are the wicked who go to hades, until the final judgment day and ultimately into hell.

As disciples today who are trying to understand the territory of the Kingdom, both now and in the future, we need some understanding of heaven because we are instructed to pray *"on earth as it is in heaven"*. The wonder of the good news is that we freely partake in this Kingdom now in the present, as well as in the future. Heaven leads us to a relationship and union with God the Father, Son and Holy Spirit, both now and more fully in the future.

Understanding the glorious future that we have in heaven should motivate us to invite as many to the wedding banquet as possible. So, let's look a little deeper into what heaven is.

Some Initial Thoughts on Heaven

God existed and heaven was created (Gen. 1:1). God simply is and he thought heaven a good place to create, so he did. God created it well, and for his own glory (Psalm 19:1). It is just perfection!

We can experience heaven on earth now, because it is the Kingdom of Heaven that Jesus ushered in and that we joined. Jesus gave us spiritual authority over this Kingdom with its keys, so that we are able to call heaven into being on this earth (Matt. 16:18-19).

Our imperishable inheritance in Christ is kept in heaven for us… *"In his great mercy, he has given us new birth into a living hope through the resurrection of Jesus Christ from the dead, and into an inheritance that can never perish, spoil or fade. **This inheritance is kept in heaven for you**"* (1 Peter 1:3-4).

What is eternal life?

First things first: gaining eternal life means that you have entered the Kingdom.

My church movement, Elim, has written its own foundational truth on what we believe the **Future State** of mankind will be… *"we believe in the resurrection of the dead and in the final judgement of the world, the eternal conscious bliss of the righteous and the eternal conscious punishment of the wicked".* In other words, we will live forever in one of two places.

In the fourth century, the foundations of the Christian faith were summarised and captured in two famous creeds. From these, I want to highlight what the Church has believed for the last sixteen-hundred years regarding eternal life and the Kingdom.

Part of the **Apostles Creed** states… "*I believe in the Holy Spirit, the holy catholic Church, the communion of saints, the forgiveness of sins, the resurrection of the body, and* **the life everlasting**. *Amen*".

Part of the **Nicene Creed** states… "*We believe also in only One, Universal, Apostolic, and [Holy] Church; in one baptism in repentance, for the remission, and forgiveness of sins;* **and in the resurrection of the dead, in the everlasting judgement of souls and bodies, and the Kingdom of Heaven and in the everlasting life**".

Eternal life is not only about the quantity of how long it will last, but it is more importantly about the quality of life and how good it will be.

We know that we already have eternal life… "*I write these things to you who believe in the name of the Son of God* **that you may know that you have eternal life**" (1 John 5:13).

Eternal life means knowing God… "*Now this is eternal life:* **that they know you, the only true God, and Jesus Christ**, *whom you have sent*" (John 17:3).

Jesus is the one who provides eternal life… "**I give them eternal life**, *and they shall never perish; no one will snatch them out of my hand*" (John 10:28).

Where is Heaven?

The **first heaven** is what we see – the sky, the clouds, our earthly atmosphere (Acts 14:17). The Greek word here for heaven is *ouranothen* which means 'sky'.

The **second heaven** is the rest – all the galaxies, universes, stars and planets that are beyond the earth's immediate atmosphere. This is the place where angels engage in spiritual warfare (Eph. 6:12). Heavenly realms, *epouranios*, meaning 'a sphere of spiritual activities'.

The **third heaven** is the abode of God located beyond the universes… *"we do have such a high priest, who sat down at the right hand of the throne of the Majesty in **heaven**"* (Heb. 8:1). Heaven mentioned here is *ouranois* meaning the 'spiritual heavens'. Remember, God is Spirit… *"God is spirit, and his worshipers must worship in the Spirit and in truth"* (John 4:24). Revelation chapters twenty-one and twenty-two speak about the New Jerusalem, the city of God, that is in the third heaven. The New Jerusalem is the eternal location of the throne of God. It was the third heaven, or *ouranon*, that Jesus ascended to after his resurrection. It is the place where we as believers will also go (Acts 1:11).

If we die before Jesus returns to earth, then our interim resurrected bodies will go to be with Jesus, and therefore with the Father also. When Jesus does return, then we would be the 'dead in Christ', who will rise first and join believers still alive on earth. Whichever category we end up in, we will together meet Jesus in the air, called the Rapture of the Church (1 Thes. 4:16-17). We will then reign with Jesus on earth and after that millennial reign (Rev. 20:1-6), will come the final Judgement (Rev. 20:7-15), after which we will live eternally with God in the New Jerusalem (Rev. 21:1-4). Some believe that the New Jerusalem will be on this earth, that is 'renewed' and God will join us and his Son here. Ultimately, it does not matter what is made new or even freshly created by God, or the exact location of our eternity…as long as we are with him.

What about Paradise?

Paradise is mentioned only three times in the NT:
*"Jesus answered him, "Truly I tell you, today you will be with me in **paradise**""* (Luke 23:43).

*"I know a man in Christ who fourteen years ago was caught up to the third heaven. Whether it was in the body or out of the body I do not know—God knows. And I know that this man—whether in the body or apart from the body I do not know, but God knows—was caught up to **paradise** and heard inexpressible things, things that no one is permitted to tell"* (2 Cor. 12:2-4).

*"Whoever has ears, let them hear what the Spirit says to the churches. To the one who is victorious, I will give the right to eat from the tree of life, which is in the **paradise** of God"* (Rev. 2:7).

The Greek word used for paradise is *paradeiso*, which is a masculine noun meaning 'a park or **a garden**'. Isn't that where it all began?

How do we get to Heaven?

There are no secret doors or special ways to enter; there is only one entry point: **Jesus is the only way to get there**… *"You* *know the way to the place where I am going." Thomas said to him, "Lord, we don't know where you are going, so how can we know the way?" Jesus answered, "I am the way and the truth and the life.* **No one comes to the Father except through me.** *If you really know me, you will know my Father as well. From now on, you do know him and have seen him""* (John 14:4-7).

"And this is the testimony, that God gave us eternal life, and **this life is in his Son"** (1 John 5:11).

We have to **truly believe and confess this belief in Jesus…** *"If you declare with your mouth, "Jesus is Lord," and* **believe in your heart** *that God raised him from the dead, you will be saved. For it is* **with your heart that you believe** *and are justified,* **and it is with your mouth** *that you profess your faith and are saved""* (Rom. 10:9-10).

We simply accept salvation as a gift of God's grace; it is not something we can buy or earn… *"For the wages of sin is death, but the* **free gift** *of God is eternal life in Christ Jesus our Lord"* (Rom. 6.23).

What Body will we have in Heaven?

The body is matter, the spirit it not. A spiritual body is real and tangible so it contains form, but will be completely empowered by the Holy Spirit… *"We will receive immortal spiritual bodies…sown in the natural raised as spiritual…so will it be with the resurrection of the dead. The body that is sown is perishable, it is raised imperishable; it is sown in dishonour, it is raised in glory; it is sown in weakness, it is raised in power; it is sown a natural body, it is raised a spiritual body"* (1 Cor. 15:42-44). Yet some do think that we will have a natural body and say that is what happened with Jesus after his resurrection (Luke 24:39). Whilst that is true, Jesus was also able to transport himself into different places going through natural matter like walls. So, it is not fully a natural body as we understand it to be in the here and now.

Ultimately, the detail does not overly matter because:
We will **belong there as citizens**… *"For our citizenship is in heaven, from which we also eagerly wait for the Saviour, the Lord Jesus Christ, who will transform our lowly body that it may be conformed to His glorious body"* (Phil. 3:20-21).

We will not only see Jesus but **we will be like him**… *"But we know that when Christ appears, we shall be like him, for we shall see him as he is"* (1 John 3:2). We will be made perfect and we will live free from the power, the penalty and the presence of sin.

Heaven is '**better by far**'… *"For to me, to live is Christ and to die is gain. If I am to go on living in the body, this will mean fruitful labour for me. Yet what shall I choose? I do not know! I am torn between the two: I desire to depart and be with Christ, which is better by far; but it is more necessary for you that I remain in the body"* (Phil. 1:21-24).

What won't be in Heaven?

Many things that are part of life as we know it now, simply will not be found in heaven. There will be no sin, fear, anxiety, anger, war, hate, sickness, poverty, injustice or impurity (Rev. 21:27), no more death, sorrow, crying or pain (Rev. 21:4), no loneliness or night (Rev. 21:25), no sun or moon (Rev. 21:23), no sea (Rev. 21:1), no marriage (Matt. 22:30), no temple (Rev. 21:22) and no-one whose name is not in the Lamb's Book of Life (Rev. 21:27). It is simply going to be incredible.

Who and what will be in Heaven?

Father, Son and Holy Spirit. That should be enough for us surely! The best part of heaven will be seeing and interacting with the Trinity face to face.

The **worship of God** in heaven will make absolutely everything we have experienced here on earth seem a dim reflection, whether that be music, prayer, art or even the most beautiful places of our current world.

People. Saints that we know will be there, but again there will be some surprises, with some expected people not making it and some unexpected folks, who actually did make it.

Heaven is an **enormous city** whose architect and builder is God (Heb. 11:10). The same **precious stones** that were placed in the Ephod, which is the breastplate that the High Priest in the OT wore (Exod. 28:17-21), are also the same stones which make up the **surrounding walls** of the New Jerusalem.

Within each of these twelve immense precious stones is a huge **pearl gate** – which is a constant reminder of the high price Jesus paid on our behalf (Rev. 21:11). Each pearl gate has an **angel** assigned to it and above each gate is the name of one of the Tribes of Israel (Rev. 21:12). Each side of the city walls is six-hundred feet (200m) thick (Rev. 21:17) and around one-thousand four-hundred miles (2,240km) long. The north, south, east and west side walls each have three of these foundational stones, therefore each stone is around four-hundred and sixty-six miles (747km) long (Rev. 21:13), every stone having an apostle's name on it (Rev. 21:14).

This city is an enormous perfect cube, fourteen-hundred miles wide by fourteen-hundred miles long by fourteen-hundred miles high (Rev 21:16). If it ends up being on this earth, then perhaps, we are no longer bound only to mere horizontal travel or the full effect of gravity. How else would we be able to see this incredible city climb fourteen-hundred miles upwards and level after level of the most beautiful and majestic architecture we have ever seen? The International Space Station orbits at around two-hundred and fifty miles above the earth, where gravity is approx. 90% compared to the surface we walk on. It is all a little hard to get one's head around, isn't it?

I recently visited the Burj Khalifa building in Dubai, the tallest building in the world. At approximately half a mile high (800m), with one-hundred and sixty-three floors, it is a staggering sight. From the bottom, it seems unbelievable that such a construction could even be built. From the top the views are amazing and my legs a little jelly-like! But heaven is about two-thousand eight-hundred times taller than this man-made building. If the ceiling heights in heaven (if ceilings even exist) are similar to what we know and understand, then that would mean around a 456,400 floor lift! The horizontal landmass is roughly equal to 1,960,000 square miles, while the UK is approximately 100,000 square miles. There is space for plenty of **rooms** in this city… *"Do not let your hearts be troubled. You believe in God; believe also in me. ² My Father's house has many* *rooms; if that were not so, would I have told you that I am going there to prepare a place for you? ³ And if I go and prepare a place for you, I will come back and take you to be with me that you also may be where I am"* (John 14:1-3).

The **main street** is made of **pure gold** (Rev. 21:21); the **glory of God will light the entire city** (Rev. 21:23); the **river of life** is there (Rev. 22:1) and the **tree of life** (Rev. 22:2). There are also **rewards** in heaven... *"Look, I am coming soon! My reward is with me, and I will give to each person according to what they have done"* (Rev. 22:12).

Now, are these images of heaven literal or metaphorical? If they are only metaphorical then they are good, but if they are literal then they are definitely very good! One thing is for sure: heaven won't be how we imagine it will be – it will be much, much more wonderful.

What will we do in Heaven?
Heaven is a place of purpose. We are going to help God run the universe. We will use our gifts to administer the new heaven and the new earth. If we have been faithful with a few things then we will be entrusted with many things (Matt. 25:14-30) or even multiple 'cities' (Luke 19:17). We will most likely worship God, walk with God, learn, serve, fellowship with others and even relax!

In Conclusion
The doctrine of the new creation certainly provides great motivation for **storing up treasure in heaven** rather than on earth (Matt. 6:19-21), doesn't it.

If there is no heaven then the Christian faith falls apart. Where would our hope be? If you do feel dissatisfied with this world, it might just be because you weren't designed to live in it as it currently is. The fall of mankind changed all that, but the hope you now have in heaven might help to explain some of your discomfort here.

Perhaps we should stop more often and make more time to **ponder heaven** because heaven is where God is and hell is where he isn't. Understanding the reality of heaven and the glorious future that we have should concrete our faith and motivate us to **invite as many as possible**!

CHAPTER SIX

Summarising the Territory of the Kingdom

How can I best summarise my current understanding of the territory of the Kingdom? I set out to answer some questions that we might commonly have about it, and I hope that I have achieved this. After introducing the Kingdom, we have seen that Matthew in his Gospel certainly focuses on the Kingdom of Heaven. Perhaps it's best to have a simple snapshot first of the main points, for quick reference. So, let's recap:

1. **Entry**: we must be born again.
2. **Where**: all around and within; **When:** it's now and in the future.
3. It is **God's sovereign rule** and it is **not the Church**.
4. Matthew uniquely uses the term the **Kingdom of Heaven.**
5. **Responses to the Kingdom of Heaven:** be prepared and equipped for the responses to sharing the Kingdom with hard, unconvinced, divided or humble hearts.
6. **What the Kingdom is like**: the seven parables in chapter thirteen, if truly understood, make us **Kingdom experts!**
   - It is a **spiritual Kingdom across this whole earth** that needs to be shared urgently (1. **wheat and weeds**).
   - The Kingdom **will grow** both around us and within us (2. **mustard seed**, 3. **yeast**).
   - The Kingdom is the thing that is of **greatest ever value** (4. **hidden treasure**, 5. **pearl**).

- You should be sharing the message of the Kingdom everywhere you go (6. **net**)
- You should share your treasures of God to help the unworthy enter (7. **house owner**)

7. The Kingdom is both **merciful** and **forgiving** (8. **unmerciful servant**).

8. The Kingdom is all about maintaining the **right heart attitude** as you serve (9. **workers in the vineyard**).

9. The Kingdom **requires a response** to the King's call on your life (10. **wedding banquet**).

10. The Kingdom **requires that you prepare** and are ready spiritually for any eventuality (11. **ten virgins**).

11. Be **faithful workers** and use the skill and abilities that God has given us (12. **talents**).

12. **Further Kingdom Concepts…**
- Childlikeness: welcome purity, trust and faith, as well obedience.
- Greatness: seek to serve Jesus humbly without seeking personal status and without using self-promotion.
- Eunuchs: the Kingdom is supremely important, so we give up our strongest desires for it.
- Woes: we must invite people into a relationship with God without placing stumbling blocks in the way.
- Where preached: to the whole world that we are also sent in to.
- Already prepared: it has waited for you a long time, so live it now.

13. **Keys:** we have each been given a key to this Kingdom and the authority in prayer to advance it, unlocking heaven on earth.

14. **A Borderless Kingdom**, in the present age, with no person better than another. Only one border will be imposed in the future age.
15. **Hell**: the absolute reality of hell should motivate us to announce the Kingdom and to change eternal destinies.
16. **Heaven**: understanding the glorious future that we have, should motivate us to invite as many as possible.

How do we describe something that is invisible and yet is also demonstrable? If we can grasp the incredible framework of it, that helps us to see both its magnitude and its magnificence. Then we are able to begin to understand, that we must be willing to sacrifice for it (as citizens), and how we are supposed to function and behave in it (by following its laws). Together, with a deep revelation of our King, we are both motivated and positioned to permeate the other kingdoms of this world with the Kingdom of Heaven. As ambassadors of Christ, we are sent out to make disciples of Jesus, who will also infuse his ethos and principles wherever they go. We do this by being living examples that intentionally model it, by praying it into an effectual reality and by spiritually demonstrating it, so that it can be witnessed by others – heaven on earth.

The wider Church is supposed to be on a mission to manifest the Kingdom of Heaven as its primary goal, through making disciples. If we focus on the latter then the former should be the result. If we manage this, then all will flourish and the Kingdom of Heaven will extend. However, the ethics of the Kingdom have to become our personal ethic and the way we live out every aspect of our lives.

The Kingdom of Heaven is God's rule on earth and not our own inward desire to rule, or to do things when we want to, and in the way we want them done. Other kingdoms attempt to pull many away from Jesus. Yet the territory of the Kingdom, still covers this whole earth and is always available to everybody.

This incredible Kingdom is conferred upon us as the greatest ever gift. Not only do we enter its **Territory**, but we also become its **Citizens** who live life's greatest possible adventure, by following its life-changing **Laws**, and even having a deep, meaningful and ongoing relationship with its **King**. It turns our thinking and living completely on its head. It is an upside-down Kingdom!

I hope and pray that I have managed to help you to see more clearly the 'Territory of the Kingdom'. It really is heavenly. Perhaps I have whetted your appetite for more, or even helped to initiate your own new journey of adventure. If you are able to see more clearly now, with a **Kingdom Perspective**, then I have done what I set out to do.

Epilogue

Knowing what we do now about the 'size and shape' of the Kingdom, we are able to see things more clearly, from a **Kingdom Perspective!** Seeing things from this standpoint of a Kingdom Perspective is one thing, but living them out can be another thing altogether.

Now that a framework of the territory of the Kingdom has been established, it is time to ponder, what this all means for me personally. Having this new vantage point is wonderful, but what changes will we need to make to apply these principles in our own daily walk with Jesus? Think, review and ponder your heart motives, then create your own action plan for change. Doing so will show you how you must now live differently, and give you a way to see how are you are progressing. It does mean that you will now have to continually reach out and grab hold of the Kingdom of Heaven, and to share it with others.

Being a disciple of Jesus means an active participation in his Kingdom of Heaven, otherwise we cannot be salt and light. Inner righteousness is attainable now, but it is not perfection, not until we are made perfect in the future, when the fullness of the Kingdom of Heaven one day transpires.

Therefore, looking ahead, we are going to need to consider the personal cost of living in this Kingdom of Heaven, that we now more clearly perceive. Living as a disciple of Jesus is costly, very costly. So stay tuned, next up we will venture into the true cost of discipleship in…**Citizens of the Kingdom**!

Bibliography

Books

Barclay, W. The Gospel of Matthew Vol. 1. Edinburgh: The Saint Andrew Press, 1962.

_____,. The Gospel of Matthew Vol. 2. Edinburgh: The Saint Andrew Press, 1960.

Berkhof, L. Systematic Theology. Edinburgh: The Banner of Truth Trust, 1958.

Black, J. Apostolic Theology. A Trinitarian Evangelical Pentecostal Introduction to Christian Doctrine. Luton: The Apostolic Church, 2016.

Boice, J. M. Foundations of the Christian Faith. A Comprehensive & Readable Theology. Downers Grove: Inter-Varsity Press, 1986.

Briggs, D. Ekklesia Rising. The Authority of Christ in Communities of Contending Prayer. Kansas City: Champion Press, 2014.

Grudem, W. Systematic Theology. An Introduction to Biblical Doctrine. Leicester: Inter-Varsity Press, 1994.

Ladd, G. E. A Theology of the New Testament. Grand Rapids: William B. Eerdmans Publishing Company, 1974.

_____,. The Gospel of the Kingdom. Popular Expositions on the Kingdom of God. Grand Rapids: WM. B. Eerdmans Publishing Co., 1959.

Lenski, R. C. H. The Interpretation of St. Matthew's Gospel. Commentary on the New Testament Series. Minneapolis: Augsburg Publishing House, 1961.

Miller, D. The Kingdom and the Power. The Kingdom of God: A Pentecostal Interpretation. Springfield: AIA Publications, 2008.

Milne, B. Know The Truth. A Handbook of Christian Belief. Leicester: Inter-Varsity Press, 1982.

Slater, W. F. The Gospel of Saint Matthew. The Century Bible. Edinburgh: T.C. & E.C. Jack Ltd., 1901.

Tasker, R. V. G. Matthew. An Introduction and Commentary. Tyndale New Testament Commentaries. Leicester: Inter-Varsity Press, 1978.

Thiessen. H. C. Lectures in Systematic Theology. Grand Rapids: William B. Eerdmans Publishing Company, 1979.

Turner, D. L. Matthew. Baker Exegetical Commentary on the New Testament. Grand Rapids: Baker Publishing Group, 2008.

Warrington, K. Pentecostal Theology. A Theology of Encounter. London: T & T Clark, 2008.

Willard, D. The Divine Conspiracy. Rediscovering Our Hidden Life in God. London: William Collins, 1998.

_____,. Renovation of the Heart. Putting on the Character of Christ. Nottingham: Inter-Varsity Press, 2002.

Willard, D., Black, G. The Divine Conspiracy Continued. Fulfilling God's Kingdom on Earth. London: William Collins, 2014.

Witherington, B. The Gospel of Luke. Cambridge: Cambridge University Press, 2018.

Websites

kingdomperspective.net
leonsprings.org
thearkcc.org
vitalseed.org
elim.org.uk
elimhopechurch.net
prepareinternational.org
regents-tc.ac.uk
puertaderestauracion.com
elimoasischurch.com
elim.org.uk/missions

Author Biography

Alan has been the Pastor at Elim Oasis Church, in Broadstairs, England since 2015. Having spent most of his Christian life as part of the Elim Pentecostal Church in the UK, he was then ordained as one of their ministers in 2014, after serving in numerous other Elim churches. Much of his time in ministry has been bi-vocational, working as an IT Software Consultant, alongside leading a church. He holds a BA Honours degree in Applied Theology and an MA degree in Pentecostal and Charismatic Theology, both from Regents Theological College in England.

His greatest desire is to make disciples of those who have chosen to follow Jesus. This has led him to begin this series of books, to help extend to others what he has learned from his own discipleship journey and his learning about the Kingdom, creating…**kingdomperspective.net** to make these resources available.

Alan has travelled widely and experienced mission in many nations, helping also to lead mission teams overseas, as well as hosting mission teams into the UK. He also helps by serving the Elim Missions department based in Malvern, England, both regionally and nationally.

Married to Alice, Alan is proud father to Carl married to Carly, Sasha married to Brook, and proud grandfather to four special granddaughters: Annabelle, Elowyn, Lucy and Eleanor.

Coming Soon